SHANGO

WARRIOR OF THUNDER AND FIRE

SPIRITS OF THE ORISHAS
BOOK 7

MONIQUE JOINER SIEDLAK

MONIQUE JOINER SIEDLAK

SHANGO
Warrior of Thunder and Fire

Spirits of the Orishas Book 7

Shango: Warrior of Thunder and Fire © Copyright 2025 by Monique Joiner Siedlak

ISBN 978-1-961362-79-6 (Paperback)

ISBN 978-1-961362-80-2 (Hardback)

ISBN 978-1-961362-76-5 (eBook)

All rights reserved

The content contained within this book may not be reproduced, duplicated or transmitted without direct written permission from the author or the publisher.

Under no circumstances will any blame or legal responsibility be held against the publisher, or author, for any damages, reparation, or monetary loss due to the information contained within this book, either directly or indirectly.

Legal Notice

This book is copyright protected. It is only for personal use. You cannot amend, distribute, sell, use, quote or paraphrase any part, or the content within this book, without the consent of the author or publisher.

Disclaimer Notice

Please note the information contained within this document is for educational and entertainment purposes only. All effort has been executed to present accurate, up to date, reliable, complete information. No warranties of any kind are declared or implied. Readers acknowledge that the author is not engaged in the rendering of legal, financial, medical or professional advice. The content within this book has been derived from various sources. Please consult a licensed professional before attempting any techniques outlined in this book.

By reading this document, the reader agrees that under no circumstances is the author responsible for any losses, direct or indirect, that are incurred as a result of the use of the information contained within this document, including, but not limited to, errors, omissions, or inaccuracies.

Book Cover Design by Inkspire Designs

Published by Oshun Publications

9 Old Kings Road Suite 123 #1038; Palm Coast, FL 32137

www.oshunpublications.com

SPIRITS OF THE ORISHAS SERIES

Spirits of the Orishas: Myths of Power and Magic invites you into a world where the divine and mortal realms intertwine. This captivating series delves into the ancient tales of the Orishas, the powerful spirits of the Yoruba tradition.

Yemaya: Divine Mother of the Ocean

Oya: Goddess of Storms and Transformation

Elegua: Keeper of Crossroads and Destiny

Ogun: Blacksmith of Destiny

Oshun: Goddess of Love and Waters

Obatala: Orisha of Purity and Power

Shango: Warrior of Thunder and Fire

CONTENTS

The Storm Begins Within	ix
1. When a King Becomes Fire	1
2. The Tools That Carry His Fire	9
3. Where Thunder Lives in Tradition	17
4. The Fire That Crossed the Ocean	25
5. A Blade in One Hand a Kiss in the Other	33
6. The Hand That Strikes for Truth	41
7. The Throne That Shakes the Heavens	49
8. Fire with a Mind and a Heart	57
9. The Fire That Transforms All Things	65
10. The Drum That Speaks His Name	73
11. Building a Home for the Storm	81
12. What the Fire Hungers For	89
13. When the Storm Walks Beside You	97
14. The Storm That Will Not Be Silenced	105
15. Becoming the Storm and the Shelter	113
Leaving Footprints in the Storm	121
Bibliography	127
Newsletter Sign Up	129
About the Author	131
Also By The Author	133

INTRODUCTION
THE STORM BEGINS WITHIN

Every storm begins with a whisper.

It might be a low rumble in the distance or the way the air feels heavy just before rain. That same feeling: charged, powerful, full of mystery, lives inside many of us. We feel it when we stand up for what's right, when we speak our truth, or when we find courage we didn't know we had. That spark inside, that bold and fiery strength, is the thunder within.

This book is about learning to listen to that thunder. It's about Shango, the Orisha of lightning, fire, justice and power. He is one of the most famous deities in Yoruba spirituality, a being whose energy burns bright across continents and centuries. But more than just a god of storms, Shango teaches us how to harness our own power wisely, how to manage our emotions, honor the truth and live with pride and integrity.

Some people meet Shango through stories passed down from elders. Others feel his presence during dance or drumming. And some discover him quietly, in moments when they must choose courage over fear. However you arrive at his flame, the purpose of this journey is the same: to understand how divine power lives within human hearts.

But this is not just about learning facts or memorizing names. It's about feeling his rhythm. When you understand Shango, you begin to understand the sacred balance between strength and compassion, pride and humility, justice and mercy.

Shango reminds us that power is not about control; it is about responsibility. Lightning can destroy, but it can also light the path ahead. In the same way, our own fire can harm or heal depending on how we use it. This book is a call to know that fire and to walk with it wisely, just as Shango does.

Meeting the One Who Walks in Flame

Imagine a king whose laughter shakes the earth. His eyes flash like lightning, his voice rolls like thunder and his steps carry the rhythm of drums that never stop beating. That is Shango.

He is often pictured wearing red and white, colors that show both his passion and purity. In one hand, he holds a double-headed axe, a symbol of power and justice. It reminds everyone that what you send into the world comes back to you, just like the twin blades. His crown blazes with energy and his dance calls storms to life. When lightning splits the sky, it is said to be his signal, a reminder that truth will always reveal itself.

But Shango is more than thunder and fire. He is charm, joy, music and movement. He loves the sound of drums, the beat of dance and the excitement of celebration. He embodies the kind of energy that inspires people to stand taller and live bolder. To follow Shango is to believe in your own strength and to use it to lift others.

Yet, he is also a complex spirit. He can be fierce when faced with lies or injustice. He can bring chaos when pride goes too far. That's because Shango teaches through balance. His fire gives warmth, but it also tests one's resolve. His storms cleanse the world but can also remind us of the cost of unchecked power.

In many stories, Shango once lived as a great king of the Oyo Empire, ruling with brilliance and might. Some say his passion and anger led to his fall, but his spirit rose again as an Orisha, a divine being who still watches over thunder, lightning and truth. From ruler to god, Shango's story shows that even in failure, there can be rebirth.

To know Shango is to understand both sides of power: the rise and the fall, the flame and the ash. He walks with fire because he has mastered it. He shows that leadership and strength are sacred only when guided by wisdom and justice.

Where Sky and Soil Remember His Name

Shango's roots reach deep into Yoruba land in present-day Nigeria. Among the Yoruba people, he is honored as one of the powerful Orisha, divine forces of nature and spirit that connect heaven and earth. The Orisha are not distant gods but living presences that help guide and protect humanity. Each one teaches lessons about life, character and purpose. Shango's domain is lightning, justice, courage and kingship.

But his story did not stay in one place. During the painful years of the transatlantic slave trade, Yoruba people were taken across the ocean to the Americas. Though many tried to erase their traditions, the spirit of Shango could not be silenced. In Cuba, he became known as Changó. In Brazil, as Xangô. In Trinidad and Haiti, he discovered new voices that blended with local faiths, Catholic saints and indigenous customs.

Wherever he traveled, his fire stayed alive. People still danced for him, played his drums and called his name when seeking justice or courage. His energy adapted, but his essence never changed. Whether in a Yoruba shrine or a Brazilian temple, the beat of

Shango's drum carries the same message: power belongs to those who live truthfully and honor the divine within.

Today, Shango's influence remains a vibrant presence worldwide. His festivals bring together generations who drum, sing and dance to celebrate not just the Orisha but the strength of a culture that refused to fade. He stands as a symbol of resilience, identity and pride. His thunder reminds us that even when oppressed, the spirit can roar louder than chains.

To honor Shango is to remember where we come from and who we can still become. His story connects the sky above and the earth below, the divine and the human, the past and the present, Africa and her scattered children.

Walking the Path That Burns Bright

The lightning that strikes twice is not a mistake; it is a message. In Yoruba wisdom, Shango's thunder is not random. It comes with purpose, shaking the world to wake those who have forgotten their own strength.

To study Shango is to examine ourselves. His archetype resides within anyone who has ever felt anger at injustice, a passion for truth, or a desire to lead with courage. He represents the fiery part of the soul that wants to make things right. But he also teaches what happens when power runs wild. Through his stories, we learn that true kingship is not about ruling others, it's about mastering ourselves.

When we explore Shango's myths and symbols, we see reflections of our own lives. His triumphs show what happens when we act with confidence and clarity. His mistakes remind us to keep our pride in check. His laughter invites us to celebrate joy even in the midst of storms. His fire lights the path of transformation, showing that destruction can lead to renewal.

This is why we journey through his archetypes: the Warrior, the Lover, the Judge and the King. Each one reveals a lesson about how to use energy, emotion and action in balance. Together, they form a map for living with strength and fairness.

To walk with Shango is not to call storms without reason, but to become a storm with purpose. It is essential to understand that thunder's sound is not just a sign of power, but also a warning, guidance and a truth.

Through the pages ahead, may you come to feel Shango not as a distant figure, but as a living teacher. His fire burns in the courage to speak up. His thunder rolls in the heart that refuses to give up. His lightning flashes in every moment of truth.

He is the storm and the calm that follows. He is the justice that arrives when least expected. And he is the flame that never dies, reminding us all that power, when guided by wisdom, can change the world.

WHEN A KING BECOMES FIRE

Every great storm begins with a spark and Shango's story is no different. Long before he ruled the skies, he walked the earth as a mighty king; bold, proud and full of fire. His voice could shake walls, his laughter filled the palace and his temper was as fierce as the storms he would one day command. Yet, behind the thunder and power lies a tale of struggle, growth and transformation.

Shango's rise is not only about glory but about learning what true strength means. Through love, mistakes and the lessons of his fall, he became more than a man; he became a force of nature, an Orisha whose lightning still reminds us of the power within truth and change. His story teaches that even in the ashes of defeat, the fire of destiny can be reborn, brighter and wiser than before.

The Mortal Who Touched the Sky

Long ago, in the powerful Oyo Empire of West Africa, a king lived whose very presence could make the earth tremble. His name was Shango. He was not born an ordinary man but one marked by destiny, gifted with the fiery energy of lightning. From his youth, people spoke of his unusual strength, his fearless nature and his love for music and dance. Even as a child, thunder seemed to follow him, echoing his moods. When he laughed, storms rolled gently across the sky. When he grew angry, lightning split the heavens.

As Shango rose to power, his rule was both admired and feared. He brought prosperity to Oyo, leading his people with courage and confidence. He was a warrior, a judge and a ruler who valued honor and strength above all else. Yet, his fire was not easily controlled. His passion for justice sometimes became pride and his love for power could burn too hot. Some stories claim he discovered a secret way to command lightning itself, summoning fire from the clouds to strike his enemies. Others say he learned to harness thunder through sacred charms and the power of words.

At first, the people celebrated his might. They believed Shango's thunder proved the heavens chose him. But as his temper grew, fear began to rise alongside his fame. Some whispered that no man should hold such power. Others said the gods had given him lightning only to test his spirit. His palace became a place of awe and tension, filled with both loyal followers and worried advisors who feared his growing pride.

One day, according to legend, Shango's anger consumed him. Some say he struck his enemies with too much force, burning even his own palace with fire from the sky. Others say that betrayal among his closest allies led to chaos and in the storm of his wrath, Oyo trembled. Realizing what his fury had done, Shango left the city in sorrow. He wandered until he reached the forest, where thunder and rain followed him like faithful companions.

There, surrounded by the voice of the storm, he faced himself. In that moment of solitude, Shango understood the truth of power; it must serve, not destroy. The fire he carried was meant to bring justice, not vengeance. As lightning split the trees around him, he disappeared into the storm. The people believed he had taken his own life out of shame, but soon after, thunder roared louder than ever before.

When they looked up at the sky, they saw lightning flash with a force greater than any they had seen before. It was said that Shango had not died at all, but had been transformed. The man who once ruled the earth had become one with the heavens. He was no longer just a king; he was now an Orisha, the divine ruler of thunder and lightning. From then on, when storms raged across the land, the people lifted their heads and cried out his name. They knew their king had ascended; his fire eternal, his justice alive in the thunder that rolled across the sky.

A Throne Shattered by Lightning

Power has always been both a gift and a test and for Shango, it was no different. The myths of his reign tell of a time when Oyo was at the height of its glory; its warriors undefeated, its markets full and its people proud to serve a king who carried the strength of thunder itself. Shango's palace gleamed with red and white banners, the colors of his fiery spirit and divine purity. Drums echoed day and night, celebrating victories and calling forth blessings from the heavens. Yet beneath all that beauty and triumph, the storm of fate was quietly building.

Shango's command over lightning made him both feared and respected. It is said that he discovered sacred charms, perhaps gifted by the Orisha of iron, Ogun, which allowed him to call fire from the sky. When enemies threatened his kingdom, he raised his staff and thunder answered. His warriors followed him into battle with songs of courage, certain that even the sky fought on their side.

But as with all great power, pride began to take root. Some stories say Shango became too confident in his strength, believing himself above the other Orishas. Others say it was jealousy among his generals that turned admiration into betrayal. Regardless of which tale one believes, the end was marked by both human weakness and divine fire.

In one version of the story, Shango's rivals tricked him into using his powers carelessly, causing lightning to strike his own palace. Flames rose high, consuming what he had built and the people fled in terror. Heartbroken, Shango realized that his fire, once meant to protect, had turned against him. In another tale, he was overthrown by those he trusted most. Fleeing into exile, he carried his pain like burning coal in his chest, understanding too late that even kings must bow to the laws of balance.

The forest became his last refuge. There, Shango wrestled not with enemies, but with himself. He called out to the heavens for forgiveness, his voice rumbling like thunder across the land. Some say he climbed a tall tree, raising his axe to the sky and vanished in a flash of lightning. Others say he entered a cave, where the fire within him burst forth so fiercely that it lit the clouds above.

After his disappearance, strange things began to happen. Storms rolled over Oyo with new power, yet no harm came to the city. Thunder boomed as if in rhythm with the drums of the palace. The priests and elders gathered, listening to the sky and they understood; Shango had not died. He had ascended.

From that day, when thunder roared, the people knew it was their king speaking. When lightning struck, they said he was showing his might. Shango had become more than a man; he was now the embodiment of justice, courage and divine power. His fall became his transformation, his fire reborn in the heavens to remind all that even through failure, greatness can rise again.

Lovers, Rivals and Divine Kin

Shango's story would not be complete without the powerful spirits who shared his life, his love and his legend. The tales of his relationships reveal not only his fiery nature but also the deep connections among the Orisha. Through his bonds with Oya, Oshun and Ogun, we see how love, rivalry and respect shape the balance of divine power.

Among all his companions, Oya stands as the most passionate and fierce. She is the Orisha of winds, transformation and the cemetery gates; the keeper of change itself. Where Shango's fire burns, Oya's winds feed the flames. Together, they are storm and thunder, a union of unstoppable forces. Oya is often called his favorite, his equal in power and spirit. She rides with him into battle, her swirling tempests clearing the way for his lightning to strike. Yet, their love is not without challenge. Both are proud, both are fierce and their tempers can clash like colliding storms. But even in their quarrels, there is creation. Their energy gives birth to renewal, reminding us that passion and chaos often walk hand in hand.

Then there is Oshun, the golden goddess of love, sweetness and rivers. She represents beauty, charm and emotional wisdom; everything soft that balances Shango's fire. Where Oya is the storm, Oshun is the calm after it. She soothes his temper with laughter and song, reminding him that strength without compassion leads to loneliness. In some stories, she teaches him humility and tenderness. In others, she competes for his attention, her jealousy a reflection of his charm. Their connection shows another side of Shango; the lover who can be gentle, the king who understands the need for balance between power and love.

Yet, no story of Shango's life would be complete without Ogun, the Orisha of iron and war. Ogun is Shango's brother in some tales, his rival in others. Where Ogun's strength lies in discipline and craftsmanship, Shango's burns with flair and charisma. They are both warriors, but their paths differ; Ogun builds, Shango commands. Some myths suggest that Ogun and Shango both loved Oya, which led to tension and conflict between them. Others describe how their respect runs deep despite rivalry, for both are protectors of truth and order. When they stand together, their combined energy represents the balance of action and will.

These intertwined stories of love and rivalry are more than dramatic tales; they are lessons about harmony and conflict within the human soul. Oya, Oshun and Ogun each draw out different parts of Shango's nature: his passion, his compassion and his strength. Through them, he learns the meaning of connection and control.

In the dance of these Orisha, we see that even divine beings struggle to find balance between emotion and duty, pride and love. Their relationships remind us that every flame needs wind to move, water to cool and iron to shape its purpose. Together, they form a sacred web; one that continues to teach us about power, partnership and the beauty of divine imperfection.

Power Worn Like a Storm Cloud

In every flash of lightning and roll of thunder, there is a reminder of power that cannot be ignored. For Shango, thunder is not only a weapon or a sign of might; it is his crown. It represents his divine authority, the mark of his transformation from mortal king to Orisha. His thunder is his voice and his lightning is his judgment. When he speaks through the sky, all of creation listens.

The double-headed axe, called *oshe*, is one of Shango's most sacred symbols. It mirrors his thunder's dual nature: destruction and protection, wrath and mercy. The two blades remind us that power cuts both ways. It can be used to build and defend, or it can be used destructively when misused. The axe rests atop his crown or is carried by his devotees to show their devotion to balance and justice. In every temple where he is honored, the *oshe* stands as a reminder that leadership demands both strength and fairness.

Thunder also symbolizes Shango's royal spirit. In Yoruba tradition, kings are seen as living bridges between the divine and human worlds. When Shango ruled Oyo, his people believed he carried the energy of *Ashe*, the sacred life force that allows words and actions to shape reality. His thunder became proof of that power, the sound of divine authority moving through human will. Even after his ascension, the storms that bear his name continue to echo that truth: rightful power must come from alignment with spirit, not pride alone.

Red and white, the colors of Shango, also express the meaning of his crown. Red stands for fire, courage and passion; the heat of his energy. White represents purity, justice and clarity; the light that guides his flame. Together, they show that true kingship is a balance of both heart and wisdom. To wear Shango's colors is to carry the reminder that greatness comes from inner harmony, not domination.

When thunder rumbles across the sky, the Yoruba say it is Shango riding forth, his presence filling the air with authority and truth. His storms are not random displays of force; they cleanse, awaken and remind people to live rightly. Thunder becomes a royal decree, a voice of correction or blessing depending on one's deeds. To those who live justly, it is protection. To those who lie or harm others, it is a warning.

Shango's crown, then, is not made of gold or jewels but of storm clouds and light. It is the symbol of earned power; the kind that is both feared and respected because it serves something greater than itself. His thunder teaches that leadership is sacred work, not privilege. A crown should never rest on a head that forgets compassion or justice.

Every time lightning splits the sky, it is said that Shango is reminding humanity of what true power means. His thunder is not just noise; it is wisdom in motion. To walk with Shango is to wear your own invisible crown, guided by truth, courage and the flame of divine purpose.

THE TOOLS THAT CARRY HIS FIRE

Every Orisha carries signs that speak their language and for Shango, those symbols burn bright with meaning. His emblems are not just decorations; they are living reminders of who he is and what he stands for. The sound of drums, the flash of lightning, the gleam of a double-headed axe; each tells a story about courage, justice and divine power.

Through these symbols, Shango reveals his nature as both ruler and warrior, as well as fire and thunder, embodying strength and balance. His colors of red and white mark the meeting of passion and purity, while the foods, numbers and animals sacred to him reflect his deep connection to life's energy. To understand these emblems is to grasp how Shango's power moves through the world. They remind us that every spark, rhythm and storm carries a message from the Orisha who turns lightning into wisdom and thunder into truth.

Weapons That Speak in Thunder

Among the many symbols that represent Shango, three stand above all others: the double-headed axe, the lightning and the sacred drums. Each one carries the heartbeat of his power, speaking of justice, rhythm and transformation. To understand these emblems is to know how Shango moves; boldly, loudly and always with purpose.

The double-headed axe, known as *oshe*, is one of the most recognized symbols of Shango. It is often carved from wood or forged in metal, its two blades pointing in opposite directions. This design carries deep meaning. It reminds us that every action has two sides; what we send out into the world will one day return to us. It also represents balance, for Shango is both protector and punisher, ruler and servant of divine justice. The axe is a crown upon his head in statues and shrines, a sign of royal authority earned through trial and wisdom. Devotees who carry or wear the *oshe* do so to invite Shango's courage into their lives and to remember that real power must always be guided by fairness.

Lightning is Shango's weapon and his message. When a storm cracks across the sky, it is said that he is speaking. The Yoruba people view thunder and lightning not as simple weather but as the living expression of divine energy. When lightning strikes, it is a moment of truth; swift, bright and impossible to ignore. Shango's lightning reminds us that truth, like fire, reveals what is hidden. It can destroy lies but also bring light to darkness. Those who follow Shango know that lightning is not to be feared but respected. It teaches that change can come suddenly and that justice may arrive unexpectedly.

The drums of Shango are just as sacred as his lightning. In Yoruba tradition, the drum is not only an instrument but a living spirit. The *bata* drum, with its rich tones and rhythm, is often played during his ceremonies to call him forth. Each beat is a conversation with the divine, each rhythm a prayer. When the drums sound, they do more than create music; they open the doorway between the human and spiritual worlds. It is through the drum that Shango dances, entering the bodies of his devotees, filling them with his energy and passion. The sound of thunder in the sky and the sound of drums on Earth are the same. Both announce his presence, both command attention.

Together, the axe, lightning and drums form the trinity of Shango's power. The axe shows his authority, lightning his divine will and drums his heartbeat that connects heaven and earth. These symbols remind us that power is not silent or hidden; it is a force that is always present. It moves, it roars, it creates. To honor Shango through these emblems is to remember that strength, when used with justice and rhythm, becomes not destruction, but creation, harmony and truth.

The Colors of Fire and Purity

The colors red and white are more than decoration in the worship of Shango; they are the language of his spirit. Every Orisha carries specific colors that express their energy and for Shango, these two shades reveal the balance that defines his nature. Red burns with fire, courage and passion. White shines with purity, clarity and truth. Together, they tell the story of a ruler who commands both the heat of the storm and the calm after it.

Red is the color of fire, blood and vitality. It represents life itself; the pulse that moves through all living things. In Shango's world, red is the color of movement and power. It calls to warriors, to those who act boldly and live with purpose. When followers dress in red or place red cloth on their altars, they invite his energy of strength and confidence. Red also reminds devotees of Shango's temper, the flame that can warm or destroy depending on how it is used. It is a lesson in control, showing that passion must serve wisdom or it will consume what it loves.

White stands beside red as its equal, not its opposite. It represents peace, purity and justice; the cool light that balances Shango's heat. White is also the color of truth and higher purpose. It cleanses and restores, guiding the fire so it burns in the right direction. When Shango's followers wear white beads or offer white foods, they are asking for clarity and fairness in their actions. They seek to live with honor, to use their power for good rather than pride.

When red and white appear together, they form a sacred harmony. In rituals, worshippers often dress in alternating patterns of the two colors, symbolizing the balance of passion and purity. The colors are also used to decorate shrines, drums and ceremonial tools dedicated to Shango. Red candles burn beside white ones, each flame representing a part of his divine nature. The red feeds the fire of courage; the white keeps it holy.

This color pairing also reflects Shango's dual path as both man and god. As a mortal king, his red showed his vitality, his command and his bold leadership. As an Orisha, his white shows the divine wisdom and justice he gained after his ascension. Together, they tell the story of transformation, from human passion to divine purpose. To wear red and white is to walk in his footsteps, striving to balance strength with fairness, action with thought and emotion with truth.

Through these colors, Shango teaches a simple but powerful lesson: power without purity leads to chaos and purity without passion leads to silence. True strength is found in the balance between the two. When red and white meet, the storm becomes sacred and the fire within us burns not to destroy, but to illuminate the path of justice and honor.

The Offerings That Feed the Flame

Every Orisha has symbols that convey their energy through nature, including animals, numbers and foods that carry their essence into the physical world. For Shango, these sacred connections reflect his fiery spirit, royal pride and deep sense of justice. They are not random choices but reflections of his essence, revealing how the divine speaks through ordinary things.

The ram is the most powerful animal associated with Shango. Strong, fearless and proud, the ram reflects his courage and leadership. In nature, rams fight head-on, never turning away from a challenge. This mirrors Shango's boldness as a warrior and ruler who faces obstacles with strength and confidence. The ram's curved horns are also symbols of authority and protection, like a crown resting upon a king's head. During rituals and festivals, images of rams often adorn altars and in traditional practices, offerings are made to honor this sacred animal. The ram reminds followers that true strength comes not from aggression but from standing firm in truth and purpose.

The number six is another emblem of Shango's divine order. In Yoruba cosmology, numbers carry spiritual vibration and six represents harmony, balance and the joining of opposites. Just as Shango balances fire and justice, passion and purity, the number six reflects the need for equilibrium in all things. His followers often arrange offerings in groups of six, such as six candles, six fruits, or six coins, to align with his energy. The number reminds devotees to act with fairness and integrity, ensuring that their inner fire burns evenly, not wildly.

Food also plays a vital role in Shango's worship. He is a spirit of pleasure, celebration and abundance and his sacred tastes reflect that joy. Apples are one of his favorite offerings, representing sweetness, beauty and vitality. When an apple is placed before his shrine, it is a gesture of gratitude for life's pleasures and the hope for continued blessings. Okra, another sacred food, connects him to the earth's fertility and the power of growth. In many traditions, spicy foods and dishes cooked with red peppers are also offered, honoring his fiery energy.

Palm oil, honey and roasted corn are other traditional offerings that please him, symbolizing wealth, warmth and transformation. These foods carry not only physical nourishment but spiritual meaning; they feed the energy of Shango himself. When shared in rituals, they remind his devotees that giving and receiving are sacred acts. Every bite, every flavor is a prayer of connection between the human and divine.

Together, the ram, the number six and Shango's favorite foods form a sacred language of devotion. Each reflects an aspect of his being: the ram for strength, the six for balance and food for joy and gratitude. Through these emblems, followers learn to live as Shango teaches: with courage, fairness and celebration. They remind us that spirituality is not only found in the clouds or temples but also in what we eat, how we act and the symbols we honor every day.

The Many Masks of the Storm

Shango is not a single face in the storm; he is many. Just as lightning can strike in countless ways, Shango's power shows itself through different forms and moods. Each aspect of him reveals a lesson about strength, balance and transformation. To know Shango fully, one must understand these faces of flame, for together they show the complete spirit of the Orisha of thunder.

One of Shango's most well-known aspects is Jakuta, meaning "the stone thrower." In this form, he is fierce and unstoppable, hurling lightning stones from the heavens to punish those who abuse their power. Jakuta represents divine justice: swift, bright and fair. His energy teaches that truth always reveals itself and that no wrongdoing can remain hidden forever. Those who honor Shango as Jakuta often call upon him for protection, to expose lies and to restore balance where injustice has taken root.

Another aspect is Obakoso, meaning "the king does not hang." This form comes from the story of Shango's fall and transformation. When people thought he had died, they soon realized that his spirit had risen higher than before. As Obakoso, he embodies victory over defeat, showing that a true king never perishes; he evolves. This aspect speaks to resilience and rebirth. Followers look to Obakoso for strength in hard times, to help them rise from loss and claim their inner power once more.

Shango also appears as Lubé, a calmer and wiser face of his nature. Here, he is not the roaring storm but the glowing ember after the rain. Lubé teaches patience, reflection and the understanding that power must rest as well as rise. Devotees honor this form when seeking balance between passion and peace, courage and compassion. It is the flame that warms rather than burns, showing that mastery of fire means knowing when to hold it steady.

In some traditions, Shango assumes aspects that draw him closer to love and charm, reflecting his relationships with Oshun and Oya. In these forms, he becomes the dancer, the lover and the bringer of joy. His fire here is creative rather than destructive; the energy that moves art, music and connection. This reminds his followers that passion is not only for battle or judgment but also for celebration and creation.

Each of these aspects: Jakuta, Obakoso, Lubé and others, exists within the same divine flame. They reveal that Shango's power is not simple or one-sided. He can rage like a storm, shine like sunlight, or smolder quietly like coals waiting to reignite. The many faces of Shango demonstrate that strength takes many forms. Sometimes it roars; sometimes it listens. Sometimes it breaks; sometimes it builds.

To walk with Shango is to honor all these sides: the fire that burns, the light that guides and the warmth that heals. For within every spark of his energy lies a reflection of life itself: ever-changing, powerful and sacred in every form.

WHERE THUNDER LIVES IN TRADITION

Before he became a symbol across oceans, Shango lived deeply in the heart of Yoruba tradition. He is not just a figure of legend, but a living presence in the spiritual life of his people. A keeper of storms who bridges heaven and earth.

Within Yoruba religion, Shango's power is both feared and loved, for he represents divine justice, courage and the energy that keeps the world in balance. His shrines, songs and ceremonies are woven into the rhythm of community life, reminding everyone that the sacred is never far away.

To honor Shango is to respect the forces of nature and the laws of truth that govern all things. Let's explore how his worship unfolds in ritual, dance and devotion, revealing how a mighty king became an eternal guardian of thunder, a protector of the righteous and a light for those who walk in strength and honesty.

A Lineage Forged in Flame

In the Yoruba worldview, the divine is not distant or hidden; it lives within the world and within each person. The universe is a living network of energy, known as Àṣe, the sacred power that flows through all creation. Every Orisha is a channel of this power, expressing one of its many forms. Among them stands Shango, a force of fire and thunder, a ruler whose authority comes not only from his human kingship but from his divine role within the cosmic order.

In Yoruba cosmology, Shango is both a historical and spiritual figure. He once ruled as a king in the Oyo Empire, but his energy was so great that it transcended the bounds of mortality. After his transformation, he took his place among the Orisha as the divine embodiment of lightning, justice and moral strength. He is both man and god; proof that human beings can rise into divine purpose when they live with courage, wisdom and integrity.

The Orisha are often seen as bridges between Òrun (the spiritual realm) and Àiye (the physical world). They guide, teach and intervene when balance is lost. Shango's role in this system is unique. He governs not only storms but the principles of justice and rightful leadership. He ensures that power remains sacred and that those who wield it are held accountable. Just as lightning strikes without warning, Shango reminds humanity that truth and fairness can appear suddenly, breaking through darkness and deceit.

In Yoruba thought, every natural force carries spiritual meaning. Thunder is not simply noise; it is Shango's voice. Lightning is not random. It is a message from him, a sign of divine presence. When storms roll across the land, they are seen as moments of connection between heaven and earth. The people listen to the thunder with reverence, understanding that the same fire that gives life can also demand respect.

Shango's connection to other Orishas deepens his role in maintaining balance. He works closely with Ogun, the Orisha of iron and war, to protect order and defend truth. With Oya, he commands the winds that move the storms, teaching that transformation often comes through turbulence. His relationship with Obatala, the Orisha of wisdom and creation, reflects his need for restraint and guidance; fire must learn from light.

In temples and shrines, Shango is honored as both a royal ancestor and a divine judge. His followers turn to him when they seek courage, justice, or leadership in times of difficulty. His priests wear red and white, the colors of his energy and dance to the sound of drums that echo thunder. Through ritual, they invite his presence, allowing the community to feel his power as both protector and teacher.

Within Yoruba cosmology, Shango stands as a reminder that leadership and justice are sacred responsibilities. His fire is the strength of truth, his thunder the rhythm of divine law. He is not only the storm that cleanses the sky but also the light that follows; proof that from chaos can come clarity and from power, purpose.

Ceremonies That Shake the Earth

To honor Shango is to move with rhythm, to let the body and spirit speak in harmony. In Yoruba tradition, his presence is called forth not through quiet prayer but through sound, movement and celebration. The festivals and sacred rites dedicated to Shango are living expressions of devotion, where drums, chants and dance open a pathway for divine power to descend. Each gesture, each beat, each flash of color becomes a form of worship, transforming the ordinary into the sacred.

The Shango Festival is one of the most vibrant events in Yoruba culture. It takes place annually in the ancient city of Oyo, where Shango once ruled as king. During the celebration, the streets fill with dancers dressed in red and white, carrying double-headed axes and beating drums that echo like thunder. The rhythm of the **bàtá** drums calls to the heavens, believed to be the language that Shango himself understands. The sound rises and falls in patterns that mirror the rumble of a storm, inviting his energy to join the celebration.

The dances performed during these rituals are more than performances; they are acts of communication. Each step carries meaning. The dancers spin and stomp, their movements fierce yet graceful, symbolizing the balance between control and passion. Some leap as if struck by lightning, embodying Shango's fiery strength. Others raise their arms like the branching lines of thunder across the sky, honoring his connection to both heaven and earth. In these moments, the boundary between the human and the divine dissolves. The dancer becomes the storm and the storm becomes the dancer.

Offerings play a vital role in the rites of Shango. His altars overflow with apples, roasted corn and foods seasoned with spice and palm oil. Drums are played in cycles, priests chant invocations and the air fills with the scent of burning candles and incense. Every sound and smell is chosen to please the Orisha of fire and thunder. These acts are not just traditions; they are exchanges of energy, affirming the bond between the community and the divine.

The climax of the festival typically occurs when possession takes place. As the drumming intensifies, a chosen devotee, frequently a priest or priestess enters a trance and Shango's spirit is said to descend into them. Their movements become stronger, their voice louder, their presence commanding. The people watch with awe, for they believe that in that moment, Shango walks among them once again. Through that sacred embodiment, he blesses the community, settles disputes and renews the moral order.

These festivals and rites remind the Yoruba people that the divine is not separate from life but woven into its rhythm. To dance for Shango is to celebrate truth, courage and justice. It is essential to remember that power, when expressed through joy and unity, becomes a transformative and healing force. Through every drumbeat and every flash of lightning, the people affirm that Shango still reigns; not only in the heavens but in every heart that dares to dance the lightning path.

Sacred Places Where Fire Rests

Shrines and temples dedicated to Shango are places where thunder finds rest—where divine fire meets human devotion. They are not only physical structures but living spaces of rhythm, reverence and renewal. In these sacred sites, the energy of the storm is contained, honored and shared, allowing devotees to connect directly with the essence of Shango. Whether in the royal city of Oyo or a modest corner altar in a modern home, each shrine serves as a bridge between earth and sky, between human need and divine power.

In traditional Yoruba lands, Shango's shrines are often found near royal compounds or within sacred groves. The *ilé Sàngó*, or "house of Shango," holds his sacred implements—the double axe, drums and stones struck by lightning, called *edun ara*. These stones are not mere relics but embodiments of his energy, said to hold the very spark of the Orisha's fire. The shrine itself is a place of power and stillness, where devotees come to seek justice, courage and balance. Offerings of kola nuts, palm oil, roasted corn and ram horns are placed with care. Red and white cloths drape the altar, symbolizing Shango's dual nature: fierce and pure, passion and order.

The most famous of these sites lies in Koso, within the ancient Oyo Empire, where legend says Shango ascended into the heavens. Pilgrims visit this area to honor him as both king and Orisha, offering prayers for strength, leadership and clarity. Each year, ceremonies renew his energy in these places—priests drum, dancers move with lightning-like precision and songs rise like thunder through the air. The sound itself becomes sacred, awakening the Orisha within and around all who listen.

Beyond Africa, the thunder never truly sleeps—it rests in the hearts and hands of those who continue his worship across the world. In

Cuba, Brazil and Trinidad, temples dedicated to *Changó* and *Xangô* hum with life. The smell of incense, the rhythm of drums and the flicker of candles transform humble spaces into royal courts. Every altar, whether elaborate or simple, carries the same purpose: to invite his presence, honor his justice and celebrate his strength.

Even personal altars—small tables covered in red cloth, crowned with candles, fruit and symbols of fire—can become powerful shrines. What matters most is not size or grandeur but sincerity. When a devotee lights a candle for Shango, the flame becomes a miniature storm, a piece of divine lightning resting quietly in human care.

In every land, where thunder sleeps, the world listens. These shrines remind us that the divine is never far away; it lives in the rhythm of prayer, in the pulse of the drum and in the fire that burns quietly behind every act of courage. Shango's temples—whether built of stone, wood, or pure devotion—stand as beacons of power, truth and sacred balance, holding the echo of thunder within their walls and within the hearts of all who kneel before the fire.

Roles of Devotees and Ritual Keepers

Those who serve Shango are more than followers; they are guardians of his flame. The priests, priestesses and devotees who dedicate their lives to him carry great responsibility, for they are the keepers of fire, justice and sacred rhythm. Their role is to ensure that the connection between the human world and the realm of the Orisha remains strong, balanced and respectful. Through them, Shango's presence continues to live in ritual, in music and in the hearts of his people.

A Shango priest, often referred to as a *Babalawo* or *Oluwo Shango*, depending on the lineage, is trained through years of study, service and initiation. This process is not merely about learning rituals but about shaping character. Those who serve Shango must master self-control, for they carry the energy of thunder itself. They are taught that fire must be respected; it can provide warmth or cause destruction. Discipline, honesty and courage are the pillars of their path. A priest of Shango must be fearless in truth but humble in spirit, embodying the same balance of power and wisdom that defines their divine king.

Priestesses and female devotees, known as *Iyanifa* or *Alagbato*, hold equally important roles. They lead ceremonies, prepare offerings and interpret the will of Shango through song, dance and divination. In many traditions, women are said to carry the spark of Oya's wind, the partner and counterpart of Shango's fire. Their work ensures that both energies remain in harmony. They are protectors of balance, reminding the community that strength and gentleness must walk hand in hand.

The daily duties of Shango's ritual keepers are filled with sacred rhythm. At dawn, they greet the rising sun with prayers, acknowledging the fire of life that burns within all beings. They tend to Shango's altar, dressed in red and white, where candles burn and offerings rest on shining plates. Each item placed before him has meaning: apples for vitality, roasted corn for abundance and palm oil for sacred warmth. Incense rises like smoke from a battlefield, carrying prayers to the heavens.

Drumming is central to their practice. The *bàtá* and *dùndún* drums are considered living beings, awakened through prayer before being played. The priests learn rhythms that call to Shango; each beat is a sacred language that honors his presence. When the drums speak, the air itself changes; people begin to dance and the Orisha is invited to enter the circle.

Ritual keepers also act as guides for the community. They mediate disputes, offer spiritual counsel and help others align their lives with justice and honor. Through divination, they seek Shango's wisdom to resolve problems and restore balance. Their role is not to command but to serve; to be a vessel for truth.

To be a priest or devotee of Shango is to live with awareness of one's own fire. It means walking with courage, speaking with honesty and leading with compassion. The priests of the fire crown remind everyone that power, when guided by faith and integrity, becomes not a burden, but a blessing that lights the way for all.

THE FIRE THAT CROSSED THE OCEAN

When the Yoruba people were taken from their homeland during the transatlantic slave trade, they carried more than memories; they carried their faith. Among the spirits who crossed the ocean with them was Shango, the thunder king whose fire could never be extinguished. Though their captors tried to erase their traditions, the followers of Shango found ways to keep his name alive. In whispered prayers, secret dances and hidden altars, his thunder still roared. Across the Caribbean and the Americas, he took on new forms and names: Changó in Cuba, Xangô in Brazil and Shango in Trinidad; yet his essence remained unchanged. He became a symbol of strength, pride and freedom, a reminder that spirit cannot be chained.

Thunder That Refused to Be Broken

When millions of Africans were torn from their homelands and forced onto ships bound for the Americas, they carried more than the pain of captivity. They carried spirit. Hidden within them were the prayers, songs and stories of their ancestors; the sacred wisdom of the Orisha. Among those divine presences was Shango, the Orisha of thunder and fire, whose power could not be silenced by chains. His energy, fierce and unbroken, traveled with his people across the dark waters, lighting the path of survival and remembrance.

The journey across the Atlantic, known as the Middle Passage, was filled with unimaginable suffering. Many lives were lost and much was stripped away. Yet, even in the depths of despair, Shango's flame endured. The Yoruba people believed that no matter where they were taken, the Orisha would follow, because a spirit cannot be confined to one land. The rumble of thunder during a storm at sea was seen as a sign; Shango was still near, watching, protecting, reminding them that power and dignity could not be taken.

When the enslaved arrived in foreign lands, they found themselves surrounded by languages, laws and religions meant to erase their identity. Still, they remembered. In quiet corners and under moonlit skies, they whispered the old names, beat drums in secret and offered what little they had to honor their gods. They disguised their rituals as Christian worship or folk dance, but beneath the surface, their ceremonies were living acts of resistance.

In Cuba, the followers of Shango kept his worship alive under the name Changó, blending their Yoruba faith with Catholic imagery to survive under colonial rule. They connected him with Saint Barbara, a figure often shown holding a sword and standing beside lightning; symbols that mirrored Shango's own. In Brazil, he became Xangô, a deity worshiped openly within Candomblé temples, where his fire and justice remain central to the faith. In Trinidad, his name stayed the same: Shango, as his followers built an entire religion around his thunder, blending African, Christian and Caribbean elements into a vibrant spiritual tradition.

Through each adaptation, his essence remained. The songs may have changed languages and the rituals may have looked different, but the heartbeat of Shango never stopped. His drums still echoed through the plantations and villages, calling for freedom, pride and unity. To the enslaved, he was more than a god; he was a symbol of resistance, a reminder that strength and justice belonged to them, even when the world said otherwise.

Across the Americas, the fire of Shango became a light in the darkness. He stood as proof that culture, faith and identity could survive even the harshest oppression. His thunder roared across oceans, whispering a truth that could not be silenced: chains may bind the body, but they cannot hold the spirit. In every place his name was spoken, Shango rose again: alive, defiant and eternal.

His Voice in Many Languages

As the Yoruba people and their descendants spread across the Americas, their gods traveled with them, taking root in new lands and languages. Shango, the mighty Orisha of thunder and fire, became a symbol that adapted yet remained unbroken. His name changed from place to place, but his power, the rhythm of drums, the flash of lightning, the voice of justice, stayed the same. Across nations and generations, he lived on as Changó in Cuba, Xangô in Brazil and as a thunderous spirit within Haitian Vodou.

In Cuba, Shango became one of the most beloved and influential Orishas in the religion known as *Santería*, also referred to as *La Regla de Ocha*. Here, African traditions were carefully hidden beneath the image of Catholic saints to protect them from persecution. Shango was paired with Saint Barbara, a Christian martyr often shown with a sword, a crown and lightning in the background; perfect symbols of his divine authority. Though the outward forms changed, his followers knew who they were truly worshiping. His songs, dances and offerings remained filled with the fire of his Yoruba origins. To this day, Santería priests and priestesses still wear his colors, play his rhythms on the *bàtá* drums and call his name in praise.

In Brazil, Shango took on the name Xangô, becoming one of the central figures in *Candomblé*, a religion that blends Yoruba, Fon and Bantu traditions. His temples, known as *terreiros*, are alive with song, dance and the deep beat of drums that summon his presence. In Brazil, Xangô is honored as the Orisha of justice and truth. He is the protector of judges, leaders and those who fight against oppression. Festivals for him are grand and filled with color; devotees dressed in red and white dance with double-headed axes and sing praises that blend Yoruba with Portuguese. Through centuries of slavery and struggle, Xangô became a symbol of dignity and resilience, teaching that power and fairness must walk together.

In Haiti, his influence can be found within Vodou, where African spirits known as *lwa* guide the living. Though he is not worshiped exactly as in Yoruba tradition, Shango's energy is reflected in spirits like Ogou, the fiery warrior who commands lightning, iron and strength. The echo of Shango's thunder can be heard in their songs of resistance and pride. The fusion of African, Catholic and indigenous beliefs created a spiritual world where Shango's essence, fire, courage and justice continued to shine under new names and forms.

Through Santería, Candomblé and Vodou, Shango's story proves that borders or languages cannot contain divinity. Whether called Shango, Changó, Xangô, or hidden in the hearts of those who remember, his fire still burns. He is the living link between continents, the shared heartbeat of a people who refused to forget their gods. Across many tongues, he speaks the same truth: power rooted in justice will always rise, like thunder answering the call of the drum.

Saints Who Wore His Shadow

When the Yoruba people were enslaved and brought to the Americas, they faced harsh punishments for practicing their traditional religions. European colonizers forced them to adopt Christianity, forbidding the open worship of their Orishas. But faith, like fire, finds a way to survive. In the face of oppression, the Yoruba people and their descendants learned to weave their old beliefs into the new religion imposed upon them. This blending, known as syncretism, became a sacred disguise; a way to honor their gods under the watchful eyes of their captors. Through this transformation, Shango found a new face among the Catholic saints.

In Cuba and other parts of the Caribbean, Shango became closely identified with Saint Barbara, one of the most revered figures in Catholic tradition. Saint Barbara is often depicted wearing red, holding a sword and standing beside a tower struck by lightning. Her story tells of courage, defiance and divine justice; qualities that mirror Shango's own essence. To the enslaved, this saint was not simply a figure from the Bible; she was Shango in disguise. When they lit candles before her statue or sang hymns in her name, they were secretly calling upon the Orisha of thunder and fire.

This blending of symbols created a faith that could survive in secret. Catholic churches became hidden temples and saints' feast days turned into celebrations for the Orisha. Shango's feast was observed on December 4th, Saint Barbara's day and it remains a major festival for his followers in Cuba and beyond. Beneath the surface of Christian devotion, the rhythm of the *bàtá* drums, the scent of offerings and the flash of red and white cloth kept his true presence alive.

In Brazil, the same transformation took place. Shango became Xangô, linked to Saint Jerome or Saint John, both of whom carried symbols of wisdom, fire, or authority. In Haiti, echoes of his thunder appeared in the spirits of the *lwa*, blending his energy with those of warriors and protectors. This merging of belief was not confusion; it was strategy and resilience. The people refused to abandon their gods; instead, they allowed them to wear new masks, ensuring their survival across centuries.

Through syncretism, Shango gained what few divine figures ever do: dual identity. He became both saint and Orisha, worshiped in churches and sacred groves alike. This blending shows the creativity and endurance of the human spirit; the ability to keep faith alive even under the weight of oppression. Shango's flame adapted without dimming, his thunder spoke through new symbols and his followers continued to feel his power.

To this day, candles burn for Saint Barbara while drums sound for Shango. Two names, two faces, one spirit. The storm that once shook the earth in Oyo now echoes through cathedrals and temples across the Americas. Through syncretism, Shango proved that divine truth cannot be erased; it only changes form, like lightning finding its way through the clouds.

The Fire That Lives in the People

Across the Atlantic, Shango's fire took on new life. Though his people had been scattered, his presence grew stronger, finding expression in song, dance and community wherever Africans built new worlds. In Brazil, Cuba, Haiti and Trinidad, Shango became more than a deity; he became a symbol of identity, pride and survival. His flame continued to burn in every drumbeat, every festival and every prayer whispered beneath the sound of thunder.

In Brazil, Shango lives on as Xangô, one of the most powerful and respected Orishas in *Candomblé* and *Umbanda*. His temples, called *terreiros*, are filled with rhythm and devotion. Red and white fabrics adorn his altars and worshippers dance to the heartbeat of sacred drums that mimic the sound of thunder. Each year, grand celebrations take place in cities like Salvador and Recife, where people honor Xangô with parades, offerings and performances that blend African, Indigenous and Portuguese influences. His image also appears in art and music, representing strength, justice and the fight against oppression. For many Afro-Brazilians, Xangô is not only a god but also a cultural ancestor; a symbol of Black dignity and resilience.

In Cuba, Shango, known as Changó, remains one of the most loved Orishas in *Santería*. His fiery spirit infuses Cuban music, particularly *bata* drumming and *rumba*. The rhythm of his name pulses through songs that praise his courage and vitality. Festivals for Changó are filled with color and movement: dancers dressed in red and white swirl in patterns that reflect the motion of lightning. Even outside the temples, his influence lives in Cuban art, theater and poetry. Changó has become a national symbol of passion, rhythm and defiance. He reminds people that the strength of the ancestors still beats within them, alive in every note and every dance step.

In Haiti, though his name is less often spoken, Shango's essence burns brightly within Vodou. His energy flows through the spirits of fire and justice, especially in the warrior *lwa* Ogou. In rituals, when lightning flashes across the sky, people recognize it as the same divine power that once guided their ancestors from West Africa. The connection between thunder and freedom runs deep in Haiti; during the revolution that freed the nation from slavery, the people called upon the spirits of war and fire for courage and strength. In that cry for liberation, Shango's spirit moved once again, hidden in new names but unchanged in purpose.

In Trinidad, Shango's worship continues openly through the *Shango Baptist* or *Orisha* faith. Ceremonies are filled with drumming, chanting and spirit possession, blending Christian hymns with Yoruba prayers. Here, Shango is both a god and a cultural hero; a figure of empowerment for the African diaspora.

Across these lands, the thunder still speaks. Whether called Shango, Changó, Xangô, or hidden within other names, his flame never died. It adapted, inspired and carried hope through centuries of struggle. In every beat of the drum and every flash of lightning, his message endures: power cannot be destroyed when it burns in truth, justice and spirit.

A BLADE IN ONE HAND A KISS IN THE OTHER

Shango is often remembered as the mighty Orisha of thunder and fire, but his power is not only found in battle; it also lives in the heart. He is both warrior and lover, fierce and tender, commanding and passionate. His strength protects, but his charm inspires. To know Shango is to understand that true power is not just about conquest or dominance; it is about love, courage and balance. His stories show that the same fire that fuels war also kindles devotion and the same voice that calls down thunder can speak words of affection. Through his relationships with Oya, Oshun and Obba, we see how Shango's heart is as complex as his storm, capable of both destruction and creation.

Fighting with Passion Loving with Power

Shango stands as one of the most captivating figures in Yoruba spirituality because he embodies both power and passion in equal measure. He is the warrior who commands lightning and the lover who conquers hearts. His strength is matched only by his charm, his thunder by his laughter. To understand Shango fully is to accept that fire has two sides; it can destroy, but it can also warm and inspire. This fierce duality makes him not only a god of storms but a teacher of balance, showing that might and tenderness can exist within the same spirit.

As a warrior, Shango is fearless. His enemies tremble at the sound of his drums, for they know that where thunder roars, justice follows. He wields his double-headed axe, the *oshe*, with purpose and precision. Each swing represents divine judgment, cutting through deceit and cowardice. Shango's battles are not fought out of greed or cruelty but out of righteousness. He defends truth, protects the weak and punishes those who misuse power. His fire burns away corruption, leaving only what is honest and strong. To those who honor him, he lends courage and determination. To those who betray fairness, he brings the storm.

Yet, Shango's fire is not only the blaze of war; it is also the flame of desire. His charm is legendary. His voice, his laughter, his presence; these draw people to him as irresistibly as lightning draws the eye. In myth, he is a lover of great passion, drawn to women who match his strength and spirit, such as Oya, Oshun and Obba. Each relationship reveals a different side of him: Oya meets his fire with wind, fierce and unyielding; Oshun soothes his flame with sweetness and grace; Obba offers loyalty and devotion, grounding his restless energy. Through these unions, Shango teaches that love, like thunder, is powerful only when balanced by respect.

This combination of warrior and lover makes Shango more than a symbol of might; he becomes a model of completeness. He reminds his followers that power is hollow without heart and love is weak without courage. His duality teaches that strength and tenderness are not opposites but partners, each giving meaning to the other. In one hand, he holds the sword of justice; in the other, the warmth of affection.

In rituals, this dual nature is celebrated through dance. Devotees move with sharp, commanding gestures that mimic battle and then shift into graceful, flowing movements that represent seduction and charm. The rhythm of the drums mirrors his heartbeat; steady, strong, but alive with emotion. Each motion honors the truth that to be powerful is not to be hard and to love deeply is not to be weak.

Shango's fierce duality calls every soul to embrace both their fire and their heart. He teaches that real strength lies not in domination, but in harmony —the ability to lead with passion, to fight with honor and to love with the same power that moves the storm itself.

Daughters of Storm and Smoke

The story of Shango is inextricably linked to the women who walked beside him: Oya, Oshun and Obba. Each of these powerful Orishas played a vital role in his life, shaping his path and revealing the many layers of his spirit. Their relationships are not tales of submission or simple romance; they are lessons in balance, emotion and divine partnership. Together, they form a sacred trinity of wind, river and hearth, each showing how love can challenge, heal and transform even the mightiest of beings.

Oya, the goddess of wind, storms and transformation, is often seen as Shango's equal. She is fierce, passionate and unpredictable; like lightning's twin. Oya rides at Shango's side when thunder cracks across the sky, her winds fueling his fire. She clears paths for his lightning to strike, turning destruction into renewal. Their relationship is one of power meeting power. They clash, they ignite, but they also create something new. Oya's presence reminds Shango that change is not weakness; it is evolution. Together, they symbolize the unstoppable force of nature, teaching that love built on strength can weather any storm.

Oshun, on the other hand, brings balance to Shango's fire. She is the Orisha of love, beauty and rivers; gentle where Oya is fierce, soothing where Shango burns. Her laughter softens his temper and her sweetness teaches him compassion. When Shango's pride grows too strong, Oshun's calm waters remind him that power without kindness becomes cruelty. Their love story speaks of harmony between passion and peace. Oshun's influence tempers Shango's intensity, helping him see that even the strongest must learn to flow rather than fight. In rituals and songs, devotees often praise them together, celebrating the union of fire and water, as well as passion and tenderness.

Obba, the devoted Orisha of the home and hearth, represents loyalty and sacrifice. Her love for Shango runs deep and steadfast, though her story carries sadness. In one myth, deceived by jealousy and competition, Obba makes a painful sacrifice to win Shango's affection, only to be cast aside. Her tale is a warning about the dangers of comparison and the pain of misunderstood devotion. Yet even in her sorrow, Obba remains noble. She embodies endurance, teaching that love, though not always returned, holds its own sacred strength.

Through Oya, Oshun and Obba, we see that Shango's story is not simply one of male dominance, but of divine balance. Each woman mirrors an aspect of his soul: Oya, his fire; Oshun, his heart; and Obba, his conscience. Their interactions reveal the complexity of love; not just its joy, but its trials, sacrifices and transformations.

In their stories, the storm becomes more than thunder and rain; it becomes the meeting of elements. Fire, wind, water and earth all dance together, teaching that true love, like nature, thrives in balance. Oya, Oshun and Obba remind us that every great power, even Shango's, needs reflection, tenderness and grounding to remain whole.

The Heat Beneath His Roar

In the stories of Shango, power is never one-dimensional. He is the Orisha of thunder and fire, but he is also the embodiment of charisma, emotion and love. His strength is not just measured in battle or command; it is measured in how he feels, how he connects and how he leads with both heart and flame. Through Shango, we learn that true masculinity is not cold or distant; it is genuine and compassionate. It is passionate, expressive and deeply human.

Many cultures often teach that strength means hiding emotion, but Shango teaches the opposite. His fire burns because he feels deeply. His laughter shakes the heavens, his anger rolls across the sky and his love inspires devotion from gods and humans alike. He does not fear emotion; he channels it. His thunder is the sound of emotion made divine; rage turned into justice, joy turned into rhythm, desire turned into creation. In his fire, there is no weakness, only the courage to feel and to act with authenticity.

Shango's passion drives everything he does. He rules with confidence and pride, but also with the awareness that power must have purpose. His intensity draws people to him, not through fear but through admiration. He is magnetic because he embodies balance; fierce in will, yet warm in spirit. This combination makes him both king and lover, warrior and artist. It shows that strength without compassion is empty and emotion without direction is wasted energy; when the two merge, power becomes sacred.

His relationships reveal this truth clearly. With Oya, he meets his match: a force who challenges him to grow beyond pride. With Oshun, he learns the value of gentleness and joy. With Obba, he witnesses the endurance of devotion. Each connection deepens his understanding of emotion as a source of strength. These lessons reflect a broader truth within Yoruba belief: that fire and feeling, action and empathy, are not opposites but partners in harmony.

For Shango, passion is a form of creative energy. It fuels music, dance and celebration. His devotees praise him not through silence but through expression; through drumming, singing and movement. To honor Shango is to embrace vitality, to live boldly and to express oneself without fear. His masculinity is open and dynamic, defined not by domination but by confidence, sensuality and integrity.

Modern followers often see Shango as a symbol for reclaiming healthy masculinity, one that values emotion, honor and responsibility alongside power. He teaches that vulnerability is not weakness; it is the spark that makes strength meaningful. His fire shows that to love deeply and lead passionately is divine, not flawed.

In Shango's world, a man is not measured by how much he conquers, but by how much light he brings. His thunder reminds us that real strength is felt, not hidden. It is the heartbeat that dares to burn brightly; to lead, to love and to live with both fire and feeling.

Desire That Burns Through Legends

Love has always been one of Shango's greatest teachers. His stories are filled with passion, desire, anger and forgiveness; each emotion burns as brightly as his lightning. To know Shango is to understand that love, like the storm, is powerful and unpredictable. It can bring rain to the earth or strike with sudden fire. Through his myths, we see that emotion is sacred, even when it is messy. His heart is both his strength and his test.

In one story, Shango's love for Oya burns with the intensity of a storm. Together they are wind and fire; two forces that cannot exist apart for long. Their union is fierce and creative, their arguments thunderous but short-lived. Oya pushes him to face his pride and temper, reminding him that even the strongest must listen to others. When they dance together, their energy fills the air with life. Their love shows that passion can transform chaos into renewal when guided by respect.

With Oshun, the goddess of rivers and sweetness, Shango's heart finds a different kind of rhythm. She is the calm that cools his flame, teaching him patience and compassion. Where Oya matches his power, Oshun softens it. Their love flows like fire meeting water, creating steam; a symbol of creation and balance. Oshun's laughter charms Shango, reminding him that joy is as important as power. In her presence, his anger fades, replaced by warmth and clarity. Their story speaks of love as a healing force, one that can tame even the fiercest thunder when touched by kindness.

The tale of Obba, however, reveals the pain that can come when love turns into competition. In her devotion, Obba tries to win Shango's affection by making a sacrifice she believes will please him, but deception leads to heartbreak. Shango, misunderstanding her act, rejects her and Obba retreats into sorrow. This myth holds profound lessons about jealousy, miscommunication and the consequences of pride. It shows that even gods can err and that true love must be built on truth, not illusion.

These stories reflect the many faces of love: its beauty, its chaos and its lessons. Shango's relationships remind us that emotion is not weakness but a path toward growth. His rage teaches about control, his charm about connection and his heartbreak about humility. The Orisha of thunder feels everything deeply and in doing so, he shows that divinity is not perfection; it is authenticity.

In rituals, Shango's dual nature is honored through dance and music. Drummers play rhythms that shift between fast and slow, representing the changing moods of love and passion. Dancers embody both strength and grace, capturing the storm's intensity and the tenderness that follows.

Through his myths of love, rage and charm, Shango reminds us that the heart's storms are not meant to be avoided. They are intended to be lived, understood and transformed. From the fire of feeling comes wisdom and from every thunderclap of emotion, a deeper kind of power is born.

THE HAND THAT STRIKES FOR TRUTH

Shango is not only the master of thunder and fire; he is the voice of justice that echoes across heaven and earth. In Yoruba tradition, his lightning is more than a natural force; it is a symbol of truth striking through darkness and deceit. As a divine judge, Shango defends the innocent, punishes wrongdoing and restores balance wherever chaos has taken hold. His storms cleanse rather than destroy, reminding us that fairness is sacred and that every action has its consequences. To call upon Shango is to invite clarity, strength and accountability. His wisdom teaches that true justice comes from integrity, not vengeance and that leadership demands both power and compassion.

Justice That Falls Like Rain

In Yoruba tradition, Shango's thunder is not random; it is divine judgment made visible. When lightning flashes across the sky, it is said that the Orisha of fire and justice is speaking; reminding humanity that truth cannot remain hidden. His storms are not simply acts of nature; they are messages, warnings and corrections. Shango's lightning strikes where falsehood thrives, where arrogance grows unchecked and where injustice harms the innocent. His power restores balance to the world, proving that even when people forget right from wrong, the universe does not.

Shango's justice is swift but fair. In myths, he is often shown as a ruler who values integrity above all else. When he was king of Oyo, he rewarded loyalty, courage and honesty, but he had no patience for deceit. He could forgive mistakes, but never betrayal. His fiery temper, though fierce, was guided by a deep sense of morality. For Shango, justice was not about punishment for its own sake; it was about restoring harmony. Just as thunder clears the air after a storm, his judgment clears the soul of corruption.

In Yoruba cosmology, balance is the foundation of the world. Every act, good or bad, creates energy that must eventually return to its source. Shango's lightning embodies that law of return. When someone acts unjustly, they disturb the balance of Àṣẹ, the divine life force that flows through all things. Shango's role is to correct that imbalance. His lightning is not vengeance but consequence, a force that reminds both gods and humans that every choice has weight.

There are stories where lightning strikes those who lie under oath or misuse sacred power. When this happens, it is said that Shango himself has judged them. His punishment is direct, for he cannot tolerate hypocrisy or cowardice. Yet, he is not cruel. His justice always carries a lesson. To those who learn and change, he offers forgiveness and renewal. His storms destroy only what must be destroyed: falsehood, pride and oppression, so that truth and honor may rise again.

In ceremonies, Shango's followers call upon him when seeking justice or protection. Drums beat in rhythm with thunder and prayers rise like smoke through the air. Offerings are made with sincerity, for Shango listens closely to the hearts of those who call his name. He does not respond to empty words but answers with truth. Devotees believe that invoking his energy brings clarity to confusion and light to hidden matters.

Through Shango, justice is revealed as both a natural and divine law. His lightning teaches that wrongdoers may hide from people but never from the Orisha. Every lie will one day face the fire of truth. His thunder is the sound of accountability, echoing through the heavens and the heart alike. To walk in his light is to live honestly, to act with courage and to remember that righteousness, like lightning, always finds its mark.

Guardian of the Righteous Path

Shango's fire is fierce against lies, but it is also a shield for those who live in truth. Among the Orisha, he stands as the defender of the innocent and the voice for those who cannot speak for themselves. His thunder not only strikes the guilty; it also roars in protection of the just. In the Yoruba tradition, Shango's role as a divine protector reminds humanity that truth and courage walk hand in hand and that justice is incomplete without compassion.

As king of Oyo, Shango was known for listening to the cries of his people. He ruled with authority but also with a sense of fairness. When the weak were mistreated, he intervened. When the innocent were falsely accused, he acted swiftly to clear their names. His reign was marked by strength, but it was his dedication to truth that made him truly great. Even after his transformation into an Orisha, that same protective spirit continues. Those who are wronged call upon him in prayer, trusting that his lightning will bring justice where human hands have failed.

In Yoruba belief, the Orisha serve as intermediaries between heaven and earth, keeping balance in both realms. Shango's energy ensures that deceit never triumphs for long. His followers believe that when someone speaks the truth and is attacked for it, Shango's fire surrounds them like armor. It may not always appear as a miracle, but it creeps in unseen ways, opening paths, exposing lies and exacting harm from those who have caused it. In this way, his justice is not only cosmic but deeply personal. He stands beside anyone brave enough to live with honesty, even when it comes at a cost.

His devotees tell many stories about moments when Shango's protection saved them. Some speak of lightning striking near wrongdoers after false accusations; others describe dreams or visions in which Shango's red and white light appeared as reassurance. These experiences remind followers that truth is not powerless, even in the face of oppression. Shango's presence gives strength to endure until justice arrives.

In ceremonies, worshippers honor Shango as the "King of Truth." Drums are played to call his attention and prayers are spoken not for revenge but for righteousness. Offerings of fruit, fire and rhythm invite his presence, for he comes where courage and sincerity dwell. He is a warrior, but his war is fought not with blood, but with revelation. His weapons are thunder and light; the forces that expose what hides in shadow.

To walk with Shango is to trust that honesty will always prevail, even if it takes time. His fire may test those he protects, but only to strengthen them. He reminds his children that justice is not about destruction, but restoration. When Shango rises in defense of the truthful, no deceit can stand. His storm cleanses, his thunder declares and his lightning lights the way for all who live by the power of truth.

How to Ask the Sky to Speak

When injustice darkens a person's path, many turn to Shango to restore truth and fairness. As the Orisha of thunder, lightning and divine judgment, he is believed to hear the cries of those who suffer from deceit, betrayal, or false accusation. Calling upon Shango for justice is not done lightly; it is a sacred act that invites his fire to intervene on one's behalf. The rituals that honor him in times of conflict are both a plea and a promise; a plea for his protection and a promise to uphold truth in one's own heart.

In traditional Yoruba practice, when someone faces injustice, a priest or devotee may perform a ceremony to invoke Shango's power. The ritual often begins with cleansing. The person seeking justice is washed with cool water and palm leaves to remove spiritual impurities. Red and white cloths are then laid out before an altar decorated with his symbols: the double-headed axe (*oshe*), candles, drums and foods he loves, such as apples, okra, or roasted corn. These colors represent the balance between passion and purity, reminding participants that justice must be pursued with both strength and integrity.

Drumming plays a vital role in these ceremonies. The *bàtá* drums, sacred to Shango, are said to speak his language. As their rhythm fills the air, it is believed that his attention is drawn to the call. The drummers play specific patterns that mimic thunder, inviting him to descend and witness the matter at hand. Songs are sung in Yoruba, praising his courage and truth. The energy in the space begins to shift, charged like the air before a storm. This moment symbolizes the gathering of divine power; the calm before lightning strikes.

In some traditions, the person seeking justice offers a written petition or speaks their grievance aloud before Shango's shrine. They promise to act honorably and not seek revenge, for Shango's fire burns both the guilty and those who misuse his name. The prayer might end with a libation of water or rum poured to the earth, representing the release of the burden into divine hands. The storm is now called, not to destroy, but to correct.

These rituals are not limited to personal disputes. In communities where Shango is honored, entire groups may pray for his intervention in matters of leadership, corruption, or social injustice. During festivals, elders and priests seek his guidance in maintaining harmony, urging leaders to govern with wisdom. His energy inspires courage in those who stand up against oppression, echoing his eternal role as the protector of truth.

To call upon Shango is to trust in the power of righteousness. His justice is not about vengeance but restoration. Those who summon him must be prepared for revelation, for his lightning exposes all things, even hidden faults. When the ritual ends and thunder rolls in the distance, devotees say it is Shango's answer; his promise that truth will rise, that lies will crumble and that justice, like lightning, will always find its mark.

Walking with Fire and Honor

To walk with Shango is to live with fire in your heart, but it must be a disciplined flame. His followers are taught that true power is not found in force or dominance but in righteousness. The Orisha of thunder and justice reminds humanity that every action, word and choice carries weight. Living with fairness and integrity is the truest way to honor him. His flame does not burn for destruction but for illumination, lighting the path of honesty, courage and moral strength.

Shango's fire represents the spark of divine truth that lives within everyone. It is the inner voice that refuses to remain silent in the face of injustice. To live in alignment with that flame means acting with integrity even when no one is watching, standing firm even when it is difficult and speaking truth even when silence would be easier. Shango's devotees believe that this kind of moral courage connects them directly to his energy. Each act of fairness becomes an offering; each honest word, a spark of thunder in the soul.

In Yoruba tradition, righteousness is not only about what one avoids; it is about what one builds. Fairness is a creative energy that sustains harmony in the world. Shango teaches that justice is not limited to punishment or judgment; it encompasses compassion, protection and balance as well. A person who lives by his principles does not seek revenge but strives to make wrongs right. Like lightning that clears the sky, truth clears the heart of resentment and fear. When one lives righteously, the storms within become a source of peace.

Shango's flame also demands self-reflection. His followers are reminded that pride can distort justice; just as uncontrolled fire can destroy rather than purify. To carry his energy responsibly, one must remain humble. The wise follower does not use Shango's name to curse or condemn but to guide and enlighten. A fire that is tended carefully gives light and warmth; a fire left unchecked brings chaos. Thus, to live by his flame is to cultivate discipline, humility and compassion alongside strength.

In daily life, this teaching extends beyond ritual. Shango's followers are expected to live honorably in their communities; to be honest in their work, faithful in their relationships and fair in their decisions. Whether in the marketplace, the family, or the wider world, they are called to act as reflections of his justice. The Yoruba proverb says, *"The Orisha bless the truthful heart."* Integrity attracts divine favor because it keeps one's *Àṣẹ*, the sacred life force, clean and powerful.

Living with fairness and integrity under Shango's guidance transforms ordinary life into sacred practice. Each decision becomes a chance to keep the fire pure, to align with truth and to walk as thunder does: strong, clear and unafraid. Shango's flame of righteousness teaches that justice begins within the self. When the fire of integrity burns brightly in one heart, its light spreads to others, turning the world itself into a temple of truth.

THE THRONE THAT SHAKES THE HEAVENS

Shango is more than a god of thunder; he is a king whose rule bridges heaven and earth. His crown is forged not from gold, but from fire, wisdom and justice. In Yoruba tradition, kingship is considered sacred, reflecting the divine order of the world. As both a historical ruler of Oyo and an eternal Orisha, Shango represents the perfect union of leadership and spirit. His story reminds us that true authority is not taken; it is earned through courage, balance and service to others. To be a leader in Shango's image is to guide with strength yet remain humble before the divine.

King of Gods and Men

In the Yoruba spiritual tradition, kingship is more than a political position; it is a sacred duty, a divine covenant between heaven and earth. The king, or Alaafin, serves not only as the head of the people but as a vessel of Àṣẹ, the spiritual power that sustains all creation. Among all rulers, none embodies this divine authority more completely than Shango. Before he became an Orisha, he ruled as the Alaafin of Oyo, a king whose command inspired loyalty and awe. His reign was marked by justice, courage and a brilliance that seemed larger than life. After his transformation into a god, Shango's kingship transcended the physical realm, making him not only a ruler of people but a ruler of principles; an eternal symbol of sacred authority.

As a divine ruler, Shango represents the ideal leader: strong yet fair, fierce yet wise. His power comes from alignment with divine truth, not personal ambition. In Yoruba cosmology, a king's authority must reflect the will of *Olodumare*, the Supreme Being and serve the good of the people. When a king abuses his power, the harmony between heaven (*Òrun*) and earth (*Àiye*) is disrupted. Shango's story, from mortal king to divine Orisha, illustrates this truth perfectly. His fall from the throne was not the end of his greatness but the beginning of his enlightenment. Through humility and reflection, he came to realize that true kingship is not about ruling others, but about mastering the self.

Shango's crown of fire symbolizes this deeper wisdom. Fire can illuminate or consume, depending on how it is used. A leader who governs with wisdom becomes a guiding light; one who rules with arrogance burns everything around him. When Shango ascended to divine status, his fire became refined; no longer the flame of pride, but the eternal blaze of justice. His crown, often depicted as the double-headed axe, represents balance and accountability. One blade stands for strength, the other for fairness, reminding all leaders that power must be tempered by righteousness.

In rituals honoring Shango, his devotees praise him as *Oba Koso*, "the king who did not die." This title reflects not only his immortality but the enduring nature of true leadership. A good ruler's influence does not fade with time; it continues through the integrity they leave behind. In Yoruba tradition, when priests or community elders invoke Shango's name, they ask for his qualities to bless those in positions of authority: courage to make hard decisions, humility to listen and wisdom to act with compassion.

Shango teaches that sacred authority carries both privilege and burden. To wear the crown of fire is to stand between the divine and the human, ensuring that both remain in harmony. The divine ruler leads not by fear, but by example. His strength protects, his justice restores and his words ignite transformation. Through Shango, we learn that leadership is not about control; it is about service, integrity and the courage to let one's inner fire shine for the good of all.

Wisdom Learned in Battle and Reign

Before Shango became an Orisha, he was a man, a ruler whose leadership shaped one of the greatest kingdoms in Yoruba history. The Oyo Empire was vast and powerful, a center of trade, culture and military strength. At its heart stood Shango, the Alaafin whose fire could inspire armies and command loyalty. Yet, his time on the throne was not without trial. His reign, filled with triumph and turbulence, became the forge in which his divine wisdom was shaped. From his years as king, we learn that true leadership is not born in comfort but in storms.

As ruler of Oyo, Shango was both feared and loved. He brought order to his realm through discipline and charisma. His warriors marched with confidence because they believed in his strength. Under his rule, Oyo flourished, expanding its borders and influence. He was known for his courage and his ability to make swift decisions. But with great power came great pressure and the same fire that drove his ambition sometimes burned too brightly. Shango's temper and pride became both his gift and his test.

Legends tell that Shango sought control over the elements themselves, calling lightning down from the sky. Whether taken literally or symbolically, this act reflects his deep desire to master all forms of power. However, mastery without humility can lead to downfall. In some versions of the story, Shango's use of lightning caused destruction and his people turned against him. In others, betrayal from within his court led to chaos. Whichever tale is told, the result is the same: Shango lost his throne but not his spirit. His fall became his awakening.

From the ruins of pride came the rise of understanding. In exile, Shango reflected on what it meant to lead; not as a ruler commanding obedience, but as a servant of divine balance. He learned that leadership is not about dominance, but about responsibility. A true leader listens as much as he commands, protects as much as he punishes and carries the weight of his people's well-being as his own. Through his trials, Shango transformed his flame of ambition into the fire of wisdom.

When he later ascended as an Orisha, the lessons of Oyo became eternal truths. His devotees look to his story as a guide for navigating leadership in any form, whether in family, community, or nation. They learn that strength must always be balanced with restraint and passion must serve purpose. Shango's storms teach that failure is not the end of greatness but a passage toward deeper understanding.

The throne of Oyo remains a powerful symbol of Shango's legacy. It represents not only power but the weight of responsibility that comes with it. Throughout his reign and his fall, Shango proved that leadership, when tested by storms, can emerge purified; like lightning breaking through the clouds, it shines brighter for having faced the darkness.

Stories of Rule and Power

Among the many Orishas of Yoruba tradition, Shango holds a unique place. He is not only a ruler among men but a ruler among gods; a king who commands respect even in the divine realm. His presence is bold and unshakable, his voice the sound of thunder itself. When Shango speaks, the heavens listen. His stories of rule and power reveal how leadership, when guided by justice and courage, becomes a sacred endeavor. Yet they also remind us that even the greatest must balance pride with wisdom, for power is a fire that must be handled with care.

In Yoruba mythology, the Orisha are a vast pantheon of divine beings, each governing a force of nature or an aspect of human life. Some bring healing; others guide love, fertility, or war. But among them, Shango stands as both warrior and king. He is often described as sitting upon a throne of flame, his double-headed axe resting beside him, his crown shining like lightning. The other Orishas respect his might, for he embodies the balance between authority and justice; the divine standard of leadership.

One story tells that after his ascension from mortal life, Shango's power grew so immense that the Orisha gathered to acknowledge him as *Alaafin Orun*, King of Heaven. Even Ogun, the fierce Orisha of iron and war, bowed in respect to his judgment, recognizing that Shango's fire carried not only strength but righteousness. He was chosen to oversee disputes among the Orisha, his thunder serving as both voice and verdict. In this role, Shango became more than a god of storms; he became the guardian of divine order.

In another tale, the Orisha sought Shango's counsel when an imbalance threatened the world. The elements clashed; water rose against fire, wind against earth; and only his wisdom could restore peace. Shango called upon Oya, the Orisha of winds and change and together they calmed the chaos. Through thunder and storm, they brought harmony once more, proving that true kingship is not domination but the power to unite.

His influence extends beyond the Orisha themselves. Humans call upon Shango in times of conflict, believing that his justice extends to both the divine and mortal realms. His devotees say that when truth is hidden, Shango's lightning will reveal it. When lies spread, his thunder will silence them. This is why he is often called *Oba Koso*, "the king who did not hang." His story reminds the faithful that truth cannot be killed, that power rooted in integrity will always rise again.

As "King of Kings," Shango's rule is eternal, not because of fear, but because of the balance he represents. His strength protects, his fire purifies and his justice restores. Among the Orisha, he reigns as a symbol of rightful power; the living flame of leadership. To honor Shango is to celebrate the divine principle that true authority serves the greater good. His throne burns brightly as a reminder that all who lead, whether human or divine, must do so with courage, fairness and unwavering truth.

Wearing the Crown in Modern Times

Though Shango's stories were born centuries ago, his lessons remain timeless. The world has changed, but the challenges of leadership, power, responsibility and integrity are still the same. In every age, people rise to positions of influence and with that comes the test of how they will use their fire. Shango's example teaches that leadership is not about domination or control, but about balance, justice and service. His crown of fire is not a reward; it is a reminder of the responsibility that comes with power.

In today's world, leaders face storms of a different kind. They may not command armies or kingdoms, but they navigate social upheaval, moral dilemmas and the expectations of those they serve. Whether they lead families, communities, or nations, Shango's principles can guide them. His life and myths remind us that strength must be matched by humility and authority must be rooted in truth. A leader who rules through fear creates silence, but one who leads with integrity creates harmony.

Modern followers of Shango see his influence everywhere: among activists who fight for justice, teachers who inspire their students and individuals who stand firm in truth despite opposition. Each act of fairness and courage echoes his thunder. His fire lives on in those who speak up against corruption, defend the powerless and take responsibility for their choices. Shango's message is that leadership begins within the self. Before one can lead others, one must rule one's own passions, temper and pride.

In a world often driven by ego and ambition, Shango's story offers an antidote. His own rise and fall as king of Oyo show that unchecked pride leads to ruin, but reflection and transformation lead to divine strength. This lesson is especially relevant for today's leaders, who must strike a balance between confidence and accountability. True leadership, as Shango demonstrates, is not about seeking personal glory but about serving something greater; whether it is a community, a cause, or a principle.

Even outside of politics or religion, Shango's teachings apply to daily life. Parents guiding their children, entrepreneurs building ethical businesses and artists using their voices for truth; all walk the path of leadership in their own way. To embody Shango's fire is to act boldly but fairly, to create rather than destroy, to speak truth even when it trembles. His thunder reminds us that silence in the face of injustice is itself a kind of false peace.

Living by Shango's example means understanding that every decision sends ripples through the world. His crown is a symbol of mindful power; one that glows brightest when guided by wisdom. In today's world, anyone can wear that invisible crown by leading with courage, standing for truth and using their fire to bring light rather than harm. To lead like Shango is to let your thunder serve the greater good and your flame illuminate the path for others.

THE FIRE THAT TRANSFORMS ALL THINGS

Shango's fire is not only a symbol of strength; it is a test of character. Power, in his hands, is sacred, but it must be guided by wisdom and restraint. The stories of Shango reveal that even divine might can become destructive when unchecked pride prevails. Yet, they also show that mercy and self-control transform strength into greatness. In Yoruba tradition, ethics are not just rules but a way of living in harmony with the universe. Shango embodies this balance: fierce but fair, passionate but just, proud yet capable of forgiveness. His lessons remind us that integrity is the crown every person must wear and that true leadership begins within.

Knowing When to Burn and When to Hold Back

Shango is the embodiment of divine power, but he is also its guardian. His fire burns brightly, yet it is not meant to consume without purpose. In Yoruba thought, power is sacred only when paired with conscience; when it serves truth rather than ego. Shango's legends remind us that pride without restraint leads to downfall, but when guided by honor, that same pride becomes a source of dignity. His story is the eternal lesson that strength must walk hand in hand with humility.

As a mortal king, Shango was known for his immense confidence. His presence commanded respect; his charisma drew people to him. He believed in his destiny so fiercely that even the gods took notice. But confidence, when left unchecked, can turn into arrogance. Some tales say his temper once brought destruction to Oyo and that his desire for control led to chaos. Yet, even in his mistakes, Shango grew wiser. His fall from power was not punishment; it was initiation. Through failure, he learned restraint, realizing that fire must be mastered before it can be harnessed to illuminate the world.

In Yoruba ethics, *iwà pèlé*, good and balanced character, is the measure of true greatness. Shango's journey reflects this ideal. Pride, in moderation, is not a sin; it is the flame that drives courage, leadership and creativity. But when pride grows too large, it burns the very foundation it was meant to protect. Shango teaches that the highest form of power is self-mastery. The king who can control his anger, the warrior who can act with fairness, the speaker who can choose silence when needed; all mirror Shango's evolution from impulsive ruler to divine judge.

Restraint is not weakness in Shango's world; it is wisdom. His lightning strikes with precision, never wasted. His thunder rolls with purpose, never hollow. This shows that true might does not require constant display; it reveals itself through discipline. Shango's followers are taught to honor his fire by controlling their own. In moments of anger, they remember that even thunder waits for the right moment to strike. His energy reminds them that passion can uplift or destroy, depending on how it is wielded.

Honor is the final thread that ties his ethics together. For Shango, integrity is sacred currency. A person's word carries power and breaking it weakens the soul. To live with honor is to live in alignment with *Àṣẹ*, the divine life force. It means acting with fairness, showing respect and standing firm in truth even when it is difficult. Shango's stories remind his devotees that dignity does not come from being feared; it comes from being trusted.

In the end, Shango's fire with a conscience is not about perfection but awareness. His legacy teaches that power, when tempered by humility and guided by justice, becomes a force for the divine. Every person carries a spark of Shango's fire within. To live with pride, restraint and honor is to tend that inner flame wisely; so it burns bright enough to inspire, yet never wild enough to destroy.

Even Gods Can Grow Wiser

Even the mightiest of the Orisha must grow and Shango's stories remind us that strength without wisdom is incomplete. Though he is the god of thunder and lightning, his journey is one of transformation; from a proud king whose fire once burned too fiercely to a divine ruler who learned mercy and balance. His myths teach that true greatness does not lie in never falling, but in learning from every mistake, rising wiser and more compassionate than before. Even thunder, with all its power, knows when to roar and when to rest.

In one well-known story, Shango's anger brings destruction to his own palace. Overcome by pride and emotion, he calls down lightning to defeat his enemies, but the storm grows beyond his control. His people flee and his kingdom trembles. Realizing the harm his fury has caused, Shango withdraws into solitude, ashamed and grief-stricken. It is in that silence, far from the noise of adoration and power, which he begins to understand himself. Fire without discipline can destroy even its master. Through reflection, he discovers that his strength was never meant to dominate, but to protect.

Another story recounts Shango's encounter with a humble farmer who a corrupt nobleman had wronged. The farmer, knowing Shango's reputation for justice, prayed for vengeance. But when Shango appeared, he saw the farmer's heart was full of hatred. Instead of striking the guilty with lightning, Shango instructed the man to forgive and let divine balance do its work. Within days, the truth came to light and the nobleman faced the consequences of his deceit. The farmer learned that mercy can achieve what rage cannot.

Through this story, Shango teaches that justice is not always about punishment; it is about restoration and healing.

Over time, these lessons shaped Shango into more than a god of storms. He became a god of transformation; a divine being who understands the power of emotion and the importance of compassion. His mercy does not come from weakness, but from mastery. Only one who has known rage can truly value peace. Only one who has wielded destruction can understand the sacred responsibility of creation.

In ceremonies, devotees honor this side of Shango through quiet prayers and acts of kindness. They light candles not only for strength, but for wisdom. They ask him to help them control their tempers, to use their words and actions for good. His fire becomes a mirror of the human heart, capable of fury, but also capable of warmth and healing.

Shango's growth reminds us that perfection is not divine; learning is. Every thunderclap carries the memory of his journey, every storm a symbol of renewal. He teaches that power gains meaning only through compassion and that mercy is the truest form of might. Through his evolution, Shango shows that even thunder learns; that every soul, no matter how fiery, can grow into grace.

Standing Between Fire and Thought

Shango is known for his fire; the thunder in his voice, the lightning in his hands and the passion that fuels his every action. Yet behind this fierce energy lies one of his greatest lessons: the balance between wrath and wisdom. His stories show that power without restraint leads to ruin, but power guided by truth becomes divine. In his journey from mortal king to Orisha, Shango learned that justice is not about the loudest strike of thunder, but about knowing when and why, to strike at all.

As a ruler, Shango was admired for his courage and strength. He defended his people with unmatched zeal, but his temper was legendary. When anger overtook him, his decisions became hasty and his storms raged beyond reason. One tale tells of a time he unleashed lightning upon his enemies, only to see innocent lives caught in the crossfire. Horrified by his own actions, he withdrew in shame, realizing that true leadership requires not only strength but discernment. It was then that he began to understand the difference between reaction and response. Wrath reacts; wisdom chooses.

Yoruba teachings remind us that emotions themselves are not wrong; it is how they are used that defines their value. Shango's fire is sacred because it moves toward balance. His anger, when righteous, becomes a tool of justice; when reckless, it becomes chaos. In this way, he reflects the very rhythm of nature: storms cleanse and nourish the earth, but unchecked, they can also destroy it. Through Shango, the Yoruba people learned that temper must serve truth, not pride.

This balance is symbolized by his double-headed axe, *oshe*, a weapon that cuts both ways. One blade represents justice, the other restraint. Together, they remind his followers that every action carries a consequence. To strike without thought harms both the target and the wielder; to hold back when justice demands action allows injustice to thrive. Shango teaches that real wisdom lies in the ability to know which path to choose; to temper passion with reflection and to act from clarity rather than fury.

In ceremonies, this lesson is embodied through rhythm. Drummers who call Shango's spirit must play with precision; too slow and the energy falters; too fast and it becomes chaos. The same is true of life. His followers strive to synchronize their heartbeat with the rhythm of his drum, learning to channel their emotions into purpose. Anger, when guided by wisdom, becomes a source of courage. Passion, when balanced with patience, becomes creation.

Shango's story encourages each person to face their own fire honestly. Suppressing anger can lead to silence and injustice, while indulging it blindly can bring destruction. The goal is mastery; a harmony between emotion and insight. His thunder teaches that sometimes justice must roar, but his silence after the storm reminds us that peace is the ultimate victory.

To live like Shango is to walk that narrow path between wrath and wisdom; to let fire reveal truth without letting it consume. His lesson endures: strength means nothing without control and power finds its highest form in the stillness that follows the storm.

Becoming the Flame That Guides Others

To walk in Shango's path is to awaken the king within; the part of the soul that rules not with ego, but with integrity. The title "king" in Yoruba tradition is not simply about authority; it is about responsibility. A king protects, uplifts and brings balance to his people. Likewise, Shango teaches that every person carries this potential within themselves; the ability to rule their own emotions, choices and actions with fairness and courage. To embody Shango's energy is to live as a just ruler of one's own life.

Shango's ethics rest on the idea that power must always serve truth. His lightning strikes to expose lies, not to display might. In the same way, his followers are called to act from honesty rather than pride. To live with ethical strength means choosing what is right even when no one is watching. It means speaking truth even when it trembles in the throat. Shango's fire burns brightest in those who do what is just because it is sacred, not because it is easy.

In Yoruba cosmology, *iwà pèlé*, or good character, is the foundation of a meaningful life. This virtue connects directly to Shango's teachings. He reminds his devotees that justice begins at home, with how one treats family, neighbors and community. To rule oneself with wisdom is to be slow to anger, quick to forgive and unwavering in truth. Every small act of fairness, whether standing up for a friend, keeping a promise, or admitting a mistake, becomes a reflection of divine order. In Shango's eyes, morality is not theory; it is practice.

His myths also teach that justice without compassion is incomplete. As a king, Shango learned that mercy can be as powerful as punishment. The wise leader knows when to strike and when to stay his hand. To those who have wronged others but seek redemption, Shango offers forgiveness through transformation. He is not a god of endless wrath, but of balance; of righting what is wrong while leaving space for growth. His sense of justice is active, not vengeful. It heals as much as it corrects.

In modern life, to embody the "just king within" means leading by example. It is found in the teacher who treats all students fairly, the parent who disciplines with love and the worker who refuses to cut corners or the leader who uses authority for the common good. Shango's lessons remind us that integrity is the true measure of success. Wealth, fame and influence fade, but character endures.

Shango's followers believe that his fire burns within every person who chooses righteousness over deceit. This inner flame, the conscience of the just king, guides us through the storms of life. To live with ethical strength is to wear an invisible crown, one forged not of gold but of truth. Through Shango's example, we learn that justice begins with self-mastery and radiates outward, transforming not only our own lives but the world around us.

THE FIRE THAT TRANSFORMS ALL THINGS

Fire has always been more than a symbol in Shango's story; it is his very essence. It burns in his laughter, his power and his truth. To the Yoruba people, fire is both a gift and a teacher, a force that gives life and demands respect. Through Shango, fire becomes sacred, representing transformation, courage and divine justice. It illuminates the path between the human and the spiritual, revealing that within every spark lies the power to transform.

The Flame That Cleanses and Destroys

Fire is one of the most powerful forces in existence; beautiful, dangerous and necessary. In Yoruba cosmology, it represents transformation, cleansing and divine energy. For Shango, fire is not just a symbol; it is his very being. It burns in his heart, dances in his storms and shines in his eyes. To understand Shango is to understand the sacred duality of fire: it can destroy, but it can also renew. It punishes falsehood yet purifies the soul. His flame teaches that every trial, every burst of anger, every moment of passion carries the potential to transform if it is guided by wisdom.

In the stories of Shango, fire always appears when truth must be revealed or change must occur. When he ruled Oyo, his fiery temper often frightened his enemies, but it also inspired loyalty. People believed that his lightning struck only when justice demanded it. In his divine form, fire became his eternal companion, representing both his fury and his gift. Shango's fire is not random; it moves with purpose. It consumes lies and lights the path for those who seek clarity.

Yoruba tradition teaches that fire, like Àṣẹ, the sacred life force, exists in all things. It is the energy that transforms one state into another, the force that turns darkness into dawn. When Shango's flame touches the world, it reminds us that transformation often requires heat. Just as metal must be forged in fire to become strong, so must the human spirit endure its own refining moments. Through anger, loss and struggle, the soul is tempered. Shango's fire challenges us to face discomfort, to confront what must change and to rise renewed.

But his fire is also fury. When injustice spreads or pride blinds the heart, Shango's temper burns bright. His storms are his voice, his lightning his command. Yet even his anger serves a purpose; it restores balance. His fury is not cruelty; it is correction. The same flame that scorches corruption also brings warmth to the righteous. In this way, Shango's fire reminds us that anger, when channeled through purpose and truth, becomes a sacred tool for change.

Ritually, fire plays an essential role in Shango's worship. Candles, torches and burning incense are lit to honor him. Devotees gaze into the flame as they pray, seeing reflections of his power within the dancing light. In ceremonies, the spark of fire symbolizes the divine presence descending into the physical world. It marks beginnings and renewals; moments when transformation is near.

To walk with Shango is to walk with the awareness that fire lives within us all. It is our passion, our conviction, our courage to speak truth. Yet, it must be tended carefully. Unchecked, it destroys; guided, it enlightens. The sacred blaze of Shango teaches that every fire has meaning. Within its heat lies not only fury but creation; the promise that from every burning comes rebirth and from every storm, the light of renewal.

Messages Written in Lightning Strikes

In the Yoruba spiritual tradition, thunder and lightning are not merely weather; they are divine communication. When the sky flashes and rumbles, it is said that Shango is speaking. His lightning is his word, his thunder his voice, echoing across the heavens to remind humanity of divine order. Through these signs, the Orisha of fire and justice delivers messages, warnings and blessings. His language is one of light and sound, understood not by the ear but by the soul.

Lightning, in Yoruba belief, is considered sacred because it embodies Àṣẹ, the divine energy that brings things into being. It is Shango's signature, the mark of his presence. Each strike of lightning is like a sentence, sharp and purposeful, spoken directly from the heavens. It can be a call to truth, a sign of protection, or a flash of revelation that exposes deceit. When lightning strikes, it is never considered random. The people say that Shango has chosen that place and that moment to speak. His power reminds all that no secret can stay hidden forever under his watchful eye.

Thunder follows lightning as the echo of divine speech. Its rumble carries authority, much like the voice of a king addressing his people. In ancient Oyo, when storms rolled through the kingdom, elders would pause their conversations, listening with reverence. They believed Shango was making his presence known, reminding them to live with honesty and courage. Even today, among Yoruba communities and in the diaspora, many still greet thunder with respect, sometimes whispering a prayer or praise in acknowledgment of the Orisha's voice.

For those who follow Shango, thunder is not a sound to fear but to honor. It teaches that words have power; that what we speak into the world creates ripples, just as thunder shakes the sky. To misuse words is to misuse Àṣẹ and Shango, as the divine judge, corrects such imbalance. His thunder warns against gossip, deceit and false witness. Just as his lightning cuts through darkness, his thunder reminds people to speak truth and act with integrity.

In ceremonies, the drum becomes a mirror of this celestial language. The *bàtá* drum's rhythms imitate the rumble of thunder, calling Shango's spirit to descend. Each beat becomes a sacred syllable, a prayer that bridges the human and divine. Devotees believe that when the drums play, they are continuing Shango's dialogue with the world, translating his heavenly thunder into earthly rhythm. Through dance, song and drumming, his followers answer his call, creating a conversation between sky and earth.

Lightning and thunder together reveal Shango's dual nature: swift and fierce, yet rhythmic and purposeful. They teach that divine power is not silent; it speaks through signs, sounds and intuition. When the heavens blaze and roar, it is not chaos but communication. Shango's thunder reminds us to listen beyond noise; to hear truth in the storm and wisdom in the rumble of creation. His language of light and sound speaks the oldest truth: that power guided by justice is the voice of the divine.

How to Speak with Smoke and Sparks

Fire has always been at the heart of Shango's worship. It is the living bridge between humanity and the divine, the element through which prayers rise and blessings descend. In Yoruba tradition and across the diaspora, rituals involving flame are central to honoring Shango. Each spark, each flicker, each column of smoke carries intention and respect. These fire-based ceremonies celebrate not only his power over lightning but also his role as purifier, protector and judge.

Before any ritual begins, devotees carefully prepare the sacred space. The altar, often draped in red and white cloth, holds offerings that please the Orisha: candles, roasted corn, apples, okra, honey and small bowls of palm oil. The air fills with the sound of drums and chants as the worshippers invoke the presence of Shango. Fire is lit not simply for light but as an invitation, signaling that the people are ready to commune with the Orisha of thunder and truth. The first flames are treated as sacred beings, living manifestations of Shango's essence.

In traditional Yoruba practice, a fire ritual may begin with prayers to *Olodumare* (the Supreme Being) and to the other Orisha, acknowledging the interconnectedness of all forces. Then, the leader of the ceremony, often a priest or priestess, calls upon Shango directly, praising his might and wisdom. The sound of the *bàtá* drums grows louder, their rhythms echoing thunder. Participants clap, sing and dance around the fire, their movements mirroring the flickering of the flames. Each step becomes a prayer in motion, a dialogue between the dancer and the divine.

Offerings are made by placing items near or into the fire, depending on the ritual's purpose. Food may be roasted as a gesture of gratitude, symbolizing transformation through heat. Incense and herbs are burned to carry prayers upward in the smoke. In some traditions, pieces of wood or paper inscribed with the names of troubles or injustices are placed into the fire, releasing them to Shango's judgment. The flame consumes what no longer serves, leaving only ashes; signs of purification and renewal.

In the diaspora, particularly in regions such as Cuba, Brazil and Trinidad, fire-based ceremonies have taken on a local flavor while retaining their spiritual essence. Candles are lit to call upon Changó or Xangô and bonfires are built during festivals to honor his strength. Dancers whirl around the flames, invoking the storm's energy, while musicians play rhythms that mimic thunder. For many, this is not mere performance but direct communion; a sacred moment when heaven and earth meet in the fire's glow.

Through these rituals, fire becomes more than an element; it becomes a catalyst for conversation, transformation and devotion. It burns away falsehood, cleanses the spirit and renews faith. Shango's worshipers understand that to offer fire is to provide truth itself. The flame listens, speaks and responds, reminding all who gather that within its light lives the power of justice, the warmth of courage and the eternal presence of the thunder king.

Turning Fire Into Freedom

Fire, in Shango's hands, is not only a force of power; it is a healer of the soul. His flame burns away what no longer serves: fear, guilt, deceit and oppression. In Yoruba thought, every human being carries both light and shadow. To live in balance, one must confront the darkness within and around them. Shango's fire gives the strength to face that darkness without being consumed by it. Through ritual, reflection and courage, his followers learn that destruction is sometimes the first step toward renewal.

Fear is one of the greatest barriers to truth. It hides justice and silences honesty. Shango's worship teaches that fear loses its grip when faced with divine fire. In ceremonies, flames are lit to represent this inner cleansing. Devotees may write down the worries or injustices that weigh upon them; betrayals, anger, guilt and feed them to the fire. As the paper burns and turns to ash, they imagine those burdens dissolving in Shango's light. The ritual is not an act of destruction, but of release. Fire transforms fear into courage, pain into wisdom.

On a larger scale, Shango's flame has long stood as a symbol of liberation. During centuries of enslavement and colonial rule, his energy became a beacon of resistance for the African diaspora. His thunderous spirit inspired courage in those who refused to accept injustice. In Trinidad, Cuba and Brazil, followers gathered in secret to invoke his strength, using fire as both a literal and spiritual weapon against oppression. Even today, his fire continues to inspire movements for truth and equality, reminding people that no force can extinguish a flame fueled by righteousness.

Shango's fire also burns through personal shadows; those hidden parts of ourselves that we fear to face. His energy demands honesty, for he cannot dwell where falsehood hides. Followers are encouraged to reflect deeply on their actions, to confront pride, anger and resentment. Just as lightning illuminates the sky for an instant, Shango's presence reveals what lies beneath the surface. Through prayer, meditation and ritual, his devotees learn that transformation begins with acknowledgment. One cannot heal what one refuses to see.

The cleansing power of fire is always balanced with compassion. Shango does not burn to destroy for pleasure; he burns to bring light. When injustice is revealed, whether in the world or the heart, it is not to condemn, but to correct. His flame teaches accountability, not cruelty. The goal is not endless judgment but renewal; a chance to begin again, purified and strong.

To walk with Shango is to carry a spark of that cleansing fire within. It is a promise to live bravely, to confront both outer and inner shadows and to keep the flame of truth alive no matter how fierce the storm. His fire reminds us that every shadow holds the possibility of light and that through courage and righteousness; even the deepest darkness can be transformed into wisdom and power.

THE DRUM THAT SPEAKS HIS NAME

Shango's fire does not reside only in stories or rituals; it is also embodied in art, music and dance. His presence is felt in the beat of the drum, the sway of the dancer, the stroke of the artist's brush and the rhythm of the storyteller's voice. Across centuries and continents, his energy has inspired countless creative expressions, carrying his thunder into the heart of culture itself. In Yoruba tradition and throughout the African diaspora, Shango's rhythm symbolizes the heartbeat of life; the pulse of truth, justice and transformation. Art becomes his language, a way for people to feel his power and celebrate his spirit.

Songs That Carry the Storm

In the world of Shango, sound is sacred. His presence is called not through silence, but through rhythm; the deep, steady pulse of drums that echoes the beat of thunder. Among the Yoruba and across the diaspora, music is the language through which Shango is praised, invoked and remembered. The drum does not simply accompany worship; it *is* worship. Its vibration carries the Orisha's energy, bridging heaven and earth, spirit and flesh. When the drums play, the air itself changes. The body begins to move, the heart quickens and the storm comes alive.

The bàtá drums are Shango's most sacred instruments. Each has a voice and together they speak in complex tones and rhythms that mirror conversation. Their beats tell stories of his strength, his fire, his justice. Drummers train for years to master these rhythms, because to play for Shango is not a performance but a prayer. The rhythms must be precise and full of respect; otherwise, they risk offending the Orisha they seek to honor. When played correctly, the *bàtá* awaken Shango's energy, inviting his spirit to descend among his devotees.

During ceremonies, music becomes the heartbeat of transformation. Dancers move in patterns that mimic lightning, sudden, sharp and radiant. Each motion is deliberate, reflecting both reverence and power. The dancers' feet strike the ground like thunderclaps and their spinning mirrors the swirling of a storm. Red and white garments flow as they move, symbolizing Shango's dual nature: passion and purity, wrath and wisdom. As the drumming intensifies, some participants enter a trance, their bodies becoming vessels for Shango's presence. In these moments, it is said that the Orisha himself dances through them, sharing his fire with all who witness.

Shango's connection to music goes beyond ritual; it extends into culture. His rhythm is rooted in the foundations of Afro-Caribbean and Latin American music, influencing genres such as rumba, salsa and samba. The *bàtá*'s thunder evolved into the beats of the conga and the call-and-response patterns of African diaspora songs. His voice echoes in the syncopated rhythms of jazz and the proud defiance of reggae and calypso. Wherever rhythm moves the soul to stand tall and speak truth, Shango's spirit can be felt.

Voice is another key aspect of his expression. In traditional Yoruba worship, *oriki*, a form of praise poetry, honors Shango's deeds and character. These poems are recited or sung, filled with metaphor and power. They describe him as the roaring sky, the breaker of lies and the flame that protects the righteous. Each verse is both devotion and declaration, reaffirming the values of courage, truth and justice.

When the drum speaks Shango's name, it reminds the people of who they are: descendants of kings, carriers of divine fire. Music and movement keep his spirit alive, not just in temples but in the hearts of those who dance, sing and drum. Every rhythm is a prayer, every movement a celebration. Through sound, Shango continues to speak, teaching that life itself is rhythm; a dance between passion and purpose, between thunder and grace.

Carving His Power into Form

The image of Shango has always been larger than life; bold, powerful and commanding. His energy is not confined to words or rituals; it is sculpted, painted, danced and performed. Through art, people give form to thunder and capture the spirit of fire. Every carving, mask, dance and performance devoted to Shango is a reflection of his divine essence. He is a god who demands to be *seen*, whose strength and rhythm inspire creativity that transcends generations.

In traditional Yoruba culture, artists serve as spiritual interpreters. When they carve or paint Shango, they do so not just to decorate, but to honor. Shango statues and masks often show him holding his double-headed axe, the *oshe*, symbolizing balance and justice. His stance is proud, his expression fierce yet composed. The symmetrical blades above his head represent the power to strike in two directions, destroying falsehood while protecting truth. These carvings, often placed in shrines or used in ceremonies, are not mere art objects; they are vessels of *Àṣẹ*, carrying the divine force that connects people to the Orisha.

Dance, too, plays a vital role in expressing Shango's thunder. The *bàtá* drums set the rhythm and the dancer becomes lightning in motion; swift, precise, unpredictable. Each gesture tells a story: a swing of the arms recalls his axe in battle; a stamping foot mimics thunder shaking the sky. Dancers wear red and white, Shango's colors and sometimes carry symbolic axes as they move in circles that represent the storm's energy. When the rhythm peaks, it is said that Shango's spirit descends into the dancer's body, merging art and divinity in a moment of sacred embodiment.

In Yoruba and diaspora communities, theater and storytelling bring Shango's myths to life. Traditional performances, which combine music, costume and movement, teach moral lessons. Plays often depict his journey from mortal king to divine Orisha, highlighting themes of pride, justice and transformation. In these stories, audiences are reminded that power must serve righteousness, which fire can both destroy and enlighten. The performances are not only entertainment; they are spiritual education, passing on ethical and cultural wisdom to new generations.

Shango's influence extends beyond Africa, shaping artistic traditions across the Americas. In Cuba, *Changó* is depicted in colorful paintings and sculptures, often crowned in flames or surrounded by drums. In Brazil, *Xangô* inspires vibrant festivals where dancers, musicians and artisans unite to celebrate his enduring power. In Trinidad, his likeness is depicted in ceremonial masks and temple art, blending African traditions with Caribbean creativity. Across these cultures, Shango's fire becomes a universal symbol of strength, justice and identity.

Art allows Shango's thunder to take form in the human world. Whether through wood, clay, movement, or voice, each creation carries his presence forward. The artist's hands, like the storm itself, are instruments of transformation. To sculpt Shango is to shape energy; to honor not just a god of lightning, but the eternal truth that beauty, passion and justice are all born from the same divine flame.

Dancing Until the Fire Rises

Wherever Shango is honored, celebration follows. His presence calls for rhythm, movement and light; a symphony of thunder expressed through human joy. Festivals dedicated to Shango are more than mere gatherings; they are sacred performances that unite community, spirit and art. Through drumming, dance, offerings and song, his devotees bring his fire to life, transforming ordinary spaces into temples of divine energy. Each festival is both worship and witness; a reminder that Shango's flame still burns brightly in the hearts of his people.

In Yoruba land, festivals for Shango often take place during the rainy season, when thunder rumbles across the sky. The timing is no coincidence. It symbolizes the union between heaven and earth, between natural storm and spiritual fire. Communities gather in open courtyards or near sacred groves, where altars decorated in red and white wait. Drummers begin the ceremony with rhythms that mimic thunder, their beats reverberating through the ground like the heartbeat of the Orisha himself. Priests and priestesses lead processions carrying torches, *oshe* axes and offerings, including bananas, corn, palm oil and roasted meat; each gift feeds the sacred flame that connects them to their divine king.

Dance is at the center of every Shango festival. The movements tell stories; his battles, his triumphs, his lessons in justice and restraint. Dancers whirl and stamp, raising dust that mixes with firelight until earth and flame seem to merge. Red and white fabrics swirl in motion, symbolizing power balanced by purity. The crowd joins in, clapping and singing *oriki*, praise songs that recount Shango's deeds and virtues. These songs are both prayer and poetry, reminding all who listen that truth and courage are eternal.

In the diaspora, Shango's festivals have adapted to new lands yet kept their spirit intact. In Cuba, the Feast of *Changó* fills the air with drumbeats, chants and bright colors. His followers wear red, light candles and dance to the rhythm of *bàtá* drums while offering apples and rum. In Brazil, *Xangô* festivals in Bahia and Pernambuco combine African, Indigenous and Portuguese influences, with celebrations that last for days, featuring parades, music and vibrant costumes. Devotees carry his symbols through the streets, affirming pride in their heritage and faith. In Trinidad, Shango Baptist gatherings blend Christian hymns with Yoruba drumming, creating a soundscape of unity between the old and the new.

Beyond their ritual meaning, these festivals strengthen community bonds. They offer a time for reconciliation, generosity and joy. Elders teach the young about Shango's values: truth, justice and courage, while artists, musicians and storytellers carry his legacy forward. The festival fire becomes a beacon, reminding everyone that life's greatest power lies in connection.

To celebrate Shango is to celebrate the divine spark within all creation. His festivals are living thunder; expressions of rhythm, justice and shared humanity. Through performance and praise, the people call down the storm not to destroy, but to renew; to let the fire cleanse, the drums speak and the community shine with the strength of the Orisha who reigns in flame and song.

Memory Kept in Movement and Song

Shango's thunder has never belonged to one land or one people; it echoes across time, carrying the strength of a culture that refused to be silenced. His worship began in the ancient city of Oyo, but through the pain of enslavement and the resilience of the African diaspora, his name spread across oceans. Wherever his followers were taken, they carried his fire within them. That fire became a spark of memory, identity and resistance. The spirit of Shango, bold, fearless and unbroken, became a living reminder that divinity cannot be chained and that cultural heritage is as enduring as thunder itself.

In the face of colonization and slavery, African traditions were often forbidden, their sacred practices labeled as dangerous or primitive. Yet Shango's people found ways to preserve their faith in secret. They sang his praises under the guise of church hymns, drummed his rhythms in the night and disguised his image beneath that of Catholic saints. In Cuba, Brazil, Trinidad and beyond, Shango took on new names, such as Changó and Xangô, but his essence remained the same. His fire became a symbol of defiance, a declaration that their spirit could not be extinguished. Every strike of lightning was a reminder from the heavens: *you are still powerful.*

Shango's energy gave courage to those who fought for freedom. His thunder was invoked in rebellion, his fire guiding revolts against injustice. In Haiti, the echoes of his power mingled with the spirits of the *lwa*, fueling the liberation struggle that gave birth to the first Black republic. In Brazil and the Caribbean, enslaved Africans and their descendants used dance and ritual as coded resistance, celebrating Shango's justice beneath the watchful eyes of oppressors. What appeared to outsiders as mere music or celebration was, in truth, an act of survival; an affirmation of identity and unity.

Over time, Shango's image evolved into a broader symbol of strength and pride for African-descended people everywhere. His fire became a metaphor for cultural endurance: the ability to adapt without losing one's essence. In modern art, music and literature, Shango continues to appear as a guardian of identity and a voice against oppression. From Afro-Brazilian drummers to Caribbean poets and African American artists, his thunder inspires creativity rooted in truth and heritage.

Today, to honor Shango is to remember one's roots. His worship keeps alive not only a spiritual connection but also a collective memory; a history of endurance, creativity and faith. Each festival, drumbeat and offering is a continuation of a story that began centuries ago. His fire still burns in those who speak out against injustice, who celebrate their roots and who walk with pride in their ancestry.

Shango's thunder will always echo wherever courage meets memory. It speaks through rhythm, art and resistance, reminding the world that culture is power, that faith is resilience and that from every storm comes the light of rebirth.

BUILDING A HOME FOR THE STORM

To honor Shango is to invite his fire into your life; not to control it, but to live in harmony with it. One of the most powerful ways to do this is by creating a sacred altar, a space where the divine and human meet. The altar serves as Shango's throne in the physical world, a place of balance, prayer and reflection. Here, candles flicker like lightning, offerings glow with gratitude and every symbol carries meaning. It is where you speak your truth, seek guidance and honor the Orisha who rules through fire and justice. Building an altar to Shango is not about decoration; it is about devotion and reverence. It represents commitment, respect and an open heart ready to receive his wisdom.

A Place Where Fire Can Rest

An altar to Shango is more than a surface adorned with candles and offerings; it is a meeting ground between the seen and unseen worlds. It is a space where the thunder's rhythm slows into silence, where divine energy becomes personal presence. For followers of Shango, the altar represents a commitment to truth, strength and balance. It is a physical reminder that spiritual life is not separate from daily life; the sacred exists wherever intention and respect are present.

In Yoruba belief, altars are extensions of the self and the home. They are not simply places to request blessings but to build relationships. Shango, as an Orisha of power, demands clarity and sincerity. To create a space for him is to invite transformation. His fire burns away pretense and his lightning illuminates the truth within. When you stand before his altar, you are standing before your own conscience. Every offering, every word spoken, carries meaning. The altar becomes a mirror, reflecting both your devotion and your character.

The importance of space in Shango's worship cannot be overstated. Just as lightning needs the open sky to strike, his energy needs sacred ground to anchor. The altar serves as that grounding point, a place where divine energy can be safely and respectfully channeled. It gives form to the intangible, allowing human hands to express reverence through touch, color and care. For devotees, tending the altar is a daily act of spiritual maintenance. Cleaning it, lighting candles and speaking prayers all reinforce a living connection between human and Orisha.

Beyond personal devotion, the altar also strengthens community and lineage. In many Yoruba households and diaspora traditions, altars are passed down through generations, carrying the prayers, wisdom and blessings of ancestors. They connect the living with those who came before; reminding each generation that spiritual power is inherited and shared. A Shango altar, in particular, calls upon not only his fiery strength but also the courage of one's ancestors who walked through storms and survived. It stands as a symbol of endurance, justice and pride.

The altar also teaches discipline and humility. Shango is not a passive deity; his presence commands respect. His followers learn that devotion is more than ritual; it is attitude. The altar demands consistency and sincerity. Neglect it and you feel the imbalance; tend it with love and it radiates peace and protection. In this way, the altar becomes a teacher, guiding the devotee toward order, mindfulness and moral clarity.

Ultimately, the altar matters because it transforms space into sacred dialogue. It is where the voice of thunder meets the whisper of the heart, where gratitude, confession and strength flow freely. To build an altar for Shango is to make a home for truth itself. It is a throne for the storm; a place where fire rests, lightning listens and the devotee remembers that within the chaos of life, there is always a center of stillness lit by divine flame.

Tools That Open the Gate to Power

Every item placed upon Shango's altar carries purpose. Nothing is chosen by chance; each symbol, color and offering speaks the language of fire and balance. To honor the Orisha of thunder is to understand that power must be approached with respect and clarity. His altar is both throne and mirror, a sacred stage where devotion meets discipline. The red cloth spread beneath his offerings becomes the foundation of that relationship; a symbol of life, passion and divine energy grounded in truth.

Red is Shango's primary color, representing fire, strength and vitality. It embodies the spark that drives action, the courage to speak and the will to lead with integrity. White, often paired with red, balances this energy with peace, purity and spiritual focus. Together, these colors express the essence of Shango's dual nature: fierce yet just, fiery yet wise. When devotees prepare his altar, they begin by laying a clean red cloth, sometimes bordered or accented with white. This foundation is not merely decorative; it marks the space as sacred, separating the physical world from the spiritual realm.

On this cloth rest the essential symbols of Shango's power. The most important is the *oshe*, his double-headed axe, representing justice and divine authority. One blade punishes wrongdoing, while the other defends the innocent. Often carved from wood and polished with care, the axe stands upright on the altar, its balance a constant reminder that power must serve fairness. Next to it may sit a carved figure of Shango himself, strong, poised and crowned with fire, reminding devotees that his strength is never without purpose.

Candles and fire are central offerings. Their flame represents Shango's living presence, illuminating truth and burning away falsehood. Lighting a candle for him is both an invitation and a declaration; a way of saying, "I seek the light of justice." Incense and cigars are also standard offerings, their smoke rising like prayers carried on the wind. Each breath of smoke is believed to please the Orisha, creating a bridge between human intention and divine awareness.

Food offerings are equally meaningful. Apples are sacred to Shango, symbolizing vitality and abundance. Roasted corn, plantains, okra and spicy dishes also honor his fiery nature. Palm oil, a sacred substance in Yoruba worship, is used to anoint his symbols or poured as a libation of gratitude. Rum or red wine may be offered in small quantities, shared in reverence before being poured to the earth as a gift to the divine.

Every offering is given with sincerity. Shango values truth above all else; he accepts no empty gestures. Before approaching the altar, devotees center themselves, speaking honestly about their intentions. Whether asking for courage, clarity, or justice, they offer with humility, knowing that the Orisha's fire reveals all hidden motives.

The altar draped in red becomes more than a place of prayer; it is a living embodiment of Shango's spirit. Each symbol, each offering, forms part of a sacred dialogue between power and purpose, reminding all who kneel before it that devotion is not only in what is given, but in how it is given; with honesty, respect and a flame in the heart.

Choosing Where the Sky Touches Earth

Creating sacred ground for Shango is an act of devotion and awareness. It is not about luxury or size; it is about intention. The altar, or *ọpọ́n Ifá*, becomes the place where thunder rests, a small yet powerful space that bridges heaven and earth. To build an altar for Shango is to declare that your home and your heart are open to his presence. Wherever it stands, that space becomes a living temple; a reminder that the divine can dwell in even the simplest corner when it is prepared with care and reverence.

The first step in creating sacred ground is choosing the location. Shango's energy is active and powerful, so his altar should occupy a place of respect, not hidden away, but not where it might be disturbed. A quiet area that allows for focus, such as a table, shelf, or stand near the east or south side of the home, is ideal, as these directions symbolize light and fire. The area should be kept clean and free from clutter, for Shango values order and dignity. Just as lightning strikes where the air is clear, his energy settles best in spaces that reflect clarity and strength.

Once the place is chosen, prepare it with intention. Cleanse the area with fresh water, herbs, or smoke from burning incense to remove any stagnant energy. Some devotees sprinkle a few drops of rum or palm wine to consecrate the space, calling upon Shango to bless it. As you prepare, speak words of invitation: simple, sincere phrases that open the path for his presence. This act is not only spiritual cleansing but also a statement of readiness; you are making a promise to honor his fire with integrity.

Next, build the foundation. Spread the red and white cloth to define the sacred space, symbolizing power and purity in harmony. On this cloth, place his symbols: the double-headed axe (*oshe*), representing justice; candles or a lamp to represent his eternal flame; and offerings that reflect his essence, such as apples, roasted corn, okra and palm oil. Some devotees add small bowls for libations, a bell or drum to call his attention, or a carved figure of the Orisha himself. Each item is chosen with purpose; never excess, never carelessness.

The altar should always feel alive. Devotees maintain it regularly, removing old offerings, wiping surfaces and refreshing the cloths and candles. Every act of care reaffirms the bond between human and divine. It is said that when the altar is neglected, the energy of the home feels heavy, but when tended with devotion, it radiates light and courage.

Finally, remember that walls do not bind sacred ground. Some followers may create a small outdoor space for Shango; perhaps beneath a strong tree or near stones that hold heat from the sun. These natural elements resonate with his essence, allowing his fire to flow freely.

To create sacred ground for Shango is to anchor thunder within the home and heart. It is a declaration of faith, a promise to live truthfully and an invitation for divine strength to dwell among you. In that space, the storm becomes peace and fire becomes light.

Feeding the Fire Every Day

Keeping the flame of Shango alive is not only about grand ceremonies; it is about consistency, reverence and heart. The fire on his altar mirrors the fire within the devotee and both must be tended regularly to remain bright. Through daily rituals, prayer and mindfulness, followers maintain a living relationship with the Orisha of thunder and justice. These practices transform ordinary moments into sacred acts, turning each day into an offering of truth, strength and gratitude.

A simple yet powerful ritual begins at dawn. The devotee greets the morning with words of respect, acknowledging Shango's light as the sun rises. Lighting a candle on the altar symbolizes awakening, renewing courage and clarity for the day ahead. As the flame flickers, a short prayer is spoken, thanking Shango for protection, guidance and justice. This act connects the heart to the Orisha's energy, reminding the follower to act with integrity in all things.

Daily devotion also includes maintaining the altar itself. Dusting, refreshing offerings and replacing spent candles are not chores; they are expressions of love and respect. In Yoruba belief, the altar is considered a living space and neglecting it can dull the spiritual connection. Keeping it clean honors not only Shango but the discipline he represents. Each act of care reinforces order, balance and accountability; the same values he expects from those who follow his path.

Prayer and song are essential parts of devotion. Devotees may sing *oriki*, praise poems that recount Shango's power and virtues, or recite personal affirmations inspired by his qualities. A few moments spent drumming, clapping, or even humming rhythmically are ways to speak his language, for Shango responds to rhythm and sound. Music awakens his presence, while silence afterward allows space for his wisdom to settle within the heart.

Shango's followers often perform small acts of justice or generosity as daily offerings. Helping someone in need, speaking truth in difficult situations, or standing up for fairness honors his spirit more deeply than material gifts. His fire burns strongest in those who live his values. Every decision made with integrity becomes a spark that keeps the flame alive in the world.

At night, the day closes as it began, with light. Before sleeping, devotees may relight a candle or softly thank Shango for the day's lessons and protection. They reflect on their actions, asking whether they lived with courage and fairness. This moment of reflection is not about guilt or perfection; it is about awareness. Shango's fire is forgiving but firm, always teaching growth through honesty.

Keeping the flame alive means living in harmony with the thunder's rhythm; balancing power with peace, passion with patience and strength with compassion. Through simple rituals and daily mindfulness, the follower becomes a vessel for his energy. Shango's fire does not fade when tended with devotion; it becomes an eternal light guiding the path toward truth, justice and the unbreakable spirit of the divine within.

WHAT THE FIRE HUNGERS FOR

To honor Shango is to celebrate the living flame; the fire that burns with truth, courage and justice. Offerings to him are not mere tradition; they are conversations with the divine, acts of gratitude and alignment with his power. Through ritual devotion, devotees connect to the essence of thunder itself, offering food, music, prayer and rhythm as symbols of respect. Each gift placed before Shango is a reflection of the heart's sincerity, for he values authenticity above all else. His fire consumes what is false and magnifies what is pure.

Rituals That Keep the Storm Awake

To feed Shango's flame is to nourish the connection between the human and the divine. Every offering, every song, every spark of light given in his name strengthens the bond between devotee and Orisha. For centuries, followers of Shango have tended his fire through ritual, acts that honor his power and invite his guidance. These ceremonies have evolved, adapting to new lands and generations, yet their purpose remains unchanged: to keep the thunder king's flame alive through devotion, gratitude and truth.

In traditional Yoruba practice, rituals for Shango are performed with great care and preparation. His ceremonies often take place outdoors or in open courtyards, where fire can move freely and thunder can be heard. The altar is dressed in red and white, his sacred colors and the air fills with the sound of *bàtá* drums; his language of rhythm and power. Offerings include apples, plantains, roasted corn and okra, along with palm oil and small portions of rum. Each item carries a meaning: the apple represents vitality, the corn symbolizes abundance, the oil signifies sacred energy and the rum represents celebration and courage. Before anything is offered, prayers are spoken to invite his presence and the devotees call his name: *Kabiyesi Shango, Oba Koso!* Acknowledging him as the king who did not die.

Fire itself is the centerpiece of these rituals. Candles, torches, or small bonfires are lit as living symbols of his energy. The flames are tended carefully, never left to burn unattended, for Shango's fire is both gift and responsibility. Devotees may dance around the fire, offering songs and rhythmic clapping to please the Orisha. In these moments, the boundary between heaven and earth fades. The drums become thunder, the dancers become lightning and Shango's spirit is said to descend among the people. His presence brings both awe and joy; a storm of transformation that cleanses the soul.

In the diaspora, Shango's rituals have evolved while retaining their essence. In Cuba, under the name *Changó*, devotees light red candles, pour libations of rum and offer dishes like spicy okra stew. In Brazil, *Xangô* is honored with grand public ceremonies featuring music, drumming and dance, where participants dress in bright red and white garments and move in rhythm with the rhythms of the storm. In Trinidad, the Shango Baptist faith combines Yoruba and Christian elements, blending hymns with ancestral drumming to honor him as both divine warrior and protector.

Contemporary followers continue to find personal ways to keep his flame alive. Some light candles at home each morning, whispering prayers for justice, courage and clarity. Others make offerings in nature, beneath trees or near stones that have felt the sun's heat, symbolizing Shango's elemental strength. Even acts of service, creativity, or truth-telling can be offerings when done with intention.

Feeding the flame is not about the quantity of gifts but the quality of devotion. Shango listens to sincerity, not spectacle. When his flame is tended with honesty, the fire does more than burn; it transforms, empowering the heart to live with the same courage, strength and passion that define the thunder king himself.

Foods That Please the Flame

Every Orisha has their favorite offerings; gifts that honor their essence and invite their presence. For Shango, the Orisha of thunder, fire and justice, these gifts are bold, vibrant and full of energy. His offerings reflect his fiery spirit, his strength as a warrior and his love of music and rhythm. Each item placed before him on the altar carries deep symbolic meaning, serving not only as tribute but as a spiritual dialogue between human devotion and divine power.

Apples are among Shango's most cherished gifts. Their round shape and bright color symbolize vitality, abundance and the sweetness of life. The apple's firmness mirrors his unwavering strength, while its flavor represents the joy that comes from living passionately and truthfully. Offering apples to Shango is a way of saying, "May my life be full of energy, courage and clarity." In many traditions, devotees polish the fruit until it gleams before placing it on his red cloth, believing that the shine pleases him and reflects his fiery pride.

Okra holds a different kind of symbolism. As a plant that thrives in heat and bears many seeds, it represents fertility, creativity and growth. Its texture and flavor align with Shango's connection to the earth and his role as a provider of nourishment. In Yoruba and diaspora traditions, okra is often cooked into spicy stews or fried dishes as offerings, seasoned with care and presented hot; never cold; to match Shango's warm, active nature. The act of cooking becomes a prayer itself, transforming simple ingredients into a vessel of devotion.

The drum, perhaps more than any other offering, is the heartbeat of Shango's worship. Its sound calls him forth, echoing the thunder that bears his voice. To gift a drum or play one in his honor is to speak his language. The *bàtá* drum, with its distinct double-headed shape, is especially sacred, symbolizing both power and balance. Drummers learn complex rhythms that praise Shango, each beat carrying history, honor and invocation. The music awakens his energy and when devotees dance to those rhythms, they are said to move as lightning incarnate. The drum is not merely an instrument; it is a living offering, a way to keep his spirit alive in every pulse of sound.

And then there is fire, his most ancient and sacred gift. Fire represents Shango himself: his courage, his passion and his justice. Lighting a candle or flame in his name is an act of reverence, a way to say, "I see your light and I keep it burning within me." The fire consumes offerings, transforming them into smoke that carries prayers to the heavens. It purifies and renews, mirroring the Orisha's dual nature: fierce yet life-giving.

Each of these gifts, apples, okra, drums and fire, honors a different aspect of Shango's being. Together, they tell his story: strength and vitality, creation and rhythm, passion and illumination. To give to Shango is not simply to offer objects but to share energy; to meet thunder with devotion and to let the divine fire within and around you burn brighter in his name.

Speaking to Him Through Rhythm

When the drums begin to beat and the voices rise in praise, it is said that Shango himself listens. The Orisha of thunder and fire is called through sound; through the rhythm of hands on drum skins, the echo of praise songs and the vibration of heartfelt prayer. His voice is the storm and his worshipers answer it with their own. In the Yoruba and diaspora traditions, words and rhythm are not just expressions of faith; they are living power, carriers of *Àṣẹ* and the divine force that makes things happen. When the community sings or prays to Shango, they are not merely honoring him; they are speaking directly to his spirit.

Prayers to Shango are often bold and full of confidence, reflecting the Orisha's fiery nature. Devotees call on him for courage, justice and protection, saying his names with reverence and strength: *Kabiyesi Shango!* Hail the King! *Oba Koso!* The King did not hang! These affirmations celebrate his triumph over death and deceit, reminding his followers that truth can never be destroyed. A prayer to Shango is not whispered timidly; it is spoken like thunder; strong, clear and alive with conviction. Worshipers may recite these words before lighting a candle, before a battle of conscience, or when asking for the strength to stand firm in truth.

Songs are at the heart of his worship. The Yoruba say that the Orisha live through music and for Shango, sound is sacred language. His songs are rhythmic and powerful, often accompanied by clapping, dancing and the *bàtá* drums. Each melody tells a story: his rise as king, his mastery over lightning, his love for Oya and Oshun, his command over justice. The call-and-response structure of many Yoruba chants mirrors the dialogue between Heaven and Earth, between the people and their divine protector. When the lead singer calls out, "Shango, bring your fire!" and the crowd responds, "Let it burn bright!" it is more than a chant; it is an invocation.

In diaspora traditions, such as Santería in Cuba and Candomblé in Brazil, these songs have evolved but retain their sacred heartbeat. *Changó* and *Xangô* are praised with songs in Spanish and Portuguese that carry the same energy as the Yoruba originals. These hymns are filled with the rhythm of the storm: driving, insistent, joyful. They invite Shango's spirit to descend and dance among his people, filling them with courage and purpose.

Drumming is the purest form of his voice. The *bàtá*, *dùndún* and *conga* drums all echo his thunder. Each rhythm carries a specific message; some call him to descend, others praise his victories, while others express gratitude for protection. Drummers are considered sacred messengers, for when they play, the Orisha listen.

Through prayer, song and rhythm, Shango's energy fills the air like electricity before rain. His voice speaks through thunder, but it also echoes in human devotion. Every beat, every verse, every breath becomes part of his eternal dialogue with the world; a reminder that faith, when spoken with truth and rhythm, can move both sky and soul.

Approaching the Thunder with Respect

Calling upon Shango is a sacred act that should always be approached with reverence, understanding and truth. The Orisha of thunder, fire and justice is powerful and direct; his energy burns bright and demands integrity. To invite his presence is to invite transformation and that requires preparation of both space and spirit. Those who walk with Shango quickly learn that honoring him properly is not about fear, but about respect. His fire blesses the honest and exposes the false. To handle his energy with honor is to remember that devotion is a partnership built on sincerity and balance.

Approach Shango with a clear and honest heart.

He is the defender of truth and will not tolerate deception, arrogance, or manipulation. Before calling him, take time to reflect on your intentions. Ask yourself why you seek his presence; are you pursuing justice, courage, or clarity? Or are you acting from pride or revenge? Shango's lightning cuts through illusion; if your motives are impure, he will reveal them, often through the lessons of experience. Honesty is the first offering he demands.

Do create order and respect in your surroundings.

Shango values strength, structure and discipline. His altar should be clean, his offerings fresh and his space free from chaos. Drumming, dancing and chanting should be performed with focus and dignity, not recklessly. Even when joy fills the ceremony, it must remain grounded in purpose. Shango's fire is joyful but disciplined; it is the rhythm of thunder, not the chaos of destruction.

Do call him with rhythm and sound.

Shango responds to vibration: the beat of drums, the clapping of hands, the voice lifted in song. Whether through the sacred *bàtá* drums or simple, heartfelt chants, his name must be spoken with confidence and rhythm. Whispering timidly will not reach him, nor will careless noise. Speak with strength, sing with devotion and let your sound carry truth.

On the other hand, there are important don'ts when invoking the Thunder King.

Don't call Shango without purpose or preparation.

His energy is not for entertainment or display. Summoning him idly can disturb spiritual balance and invite lessons you may not be ready to face. Always approach with a clear intention and after cleansing both yourself and your space.

Don't use his name for harm or manipulation.

Shango is a just and protective spirit, but he will never aid vengeance born of ego. To invoke his power for personal gain, deceit, or control over others is to misuse his fire and his lightning swiftly corrects such behavior.

Don't neglect gratitude.

Once your prayers are heard or your petition fulfilled, always give thanks through offerings, song, or acts of fairness in your own life. Gratitude keeps the spiritual bond alive and balanced.

To call Shango is to stand before the storm with faith. Handle his fire with humility, speak his name with respect and act in truth. When approached with honor, Shango answers not with punishment, but with protection, guidance and the fierce light of divine justice.

WHEN THE STORM WALKS BESIDE YOU

To walk with Shango is to carry fire in your spirit and truth in your heart. His presence is not distant or abstract; it lives within those who call upon him with sincerity. When Shango walks beside you, life becomes charged with purpose, courage and transformation. His thunder awakens the soul, urging you to speak truth, act with integrity and face challenges with strength. A personal connection to Shango is both a gift and a responsibility. It invites growth through discipline, power through balance and wisdom through experience.

Carrying His Fire in Your Chest

Calling on Shango for strength and justice is a sacred act of courage. It is a declaration that you are ready to face the truth, even when it shakes your world like thunder. Shango does not grant power lightly; he awakens it within you. When you call upon him, you are not asking for him to fight your battles; you are asking him to help you *become* strong enough to fight them yourself, guided by fairness and integrity. His fire empowers but also purifies, demanding honesty in every thought and action.

To call on Shango begins with clarity of purpose. Sit quietly before his altar or a simple candle flame and focus on what you seek. If it is strength, imagine his lightning flowing through you; bright, controlled and alive. If it is justice, speak your truth aloud, trusting that Shango hears every word spoken with sincerity. His energy moves through sound and rhythm, so clapping, drumming, or even tapping your hand against your chest while praying helps align your heartbeat with his thunder. You may say:

"Shango, king of truth, master of fire, I call upon your light.

Let your flame burn within me, guiding my words and my actions.

Where fear lives, let courage rise.

Where injustice stands, let your lightning strike to reveal truth.

Oba Koso, may your justice reign!"

The words do not need to be perfect; what matters is the heart behind them. Speak with confidence, for Shango honors boldness and authenticity.

When calling upon Shango for justice, remember that he is not a god of vengeance but of balance. His fire restores order; it burns lies and pride, but it also protects the innocent and uplifts the righteous. If you have been wronged, ask him for clarity and resolution, not destruction. If you have wronged others, call upon his light to show you the path to atonement. Justice, to Shango, is about restoring harmony; not winning a battle, but ensuring truth prevails.

Some devotees choose to make offerings during their prayers, such as apples, roasted corn, or a few drops of rum carefully poured onto the ground or into a fireproof bowl. As the smoke rises, imagine your burdens lifting with it, your intentions carried to the heavens. Others may light red and white candles to represent strength and purity, or beat softly on a drum to mimic the rhythm of rain before a storm. Each action honors Shango's essence: sound, fire and transformation.

WHEN THE STORM WALKS BESIDE YOU

To walk with Shango is to carry fire in your spirit and truth in your heart. His presence is not distant or abstract; it lives within those who call upon him with sincerity. When Shango walks beside you, life becomes charged with purpose, courage and transformation. His thunder awakens the soul, urging you to speak truth, act with integrity and face challenges with strength. A personal connection to Shango is both a gift and a responsibility. It invites growth through discipline, power through balance and wisdom through experience.

Carrying His Fire in Your Chest

Calling on Shango for strength and justice is a sacred act of courage. It is a declaration that you are ready to face the truth, even when it shakes your world like thunder. Shango does not grant power lightly; he awakens it within you. When you call upon him, you are not asking for him to fight your battles; you are asking him to help you *become* strong enough to fight them yourself, guided by fairness and integrity. His fire empowers but also purifies, demanding honesty in every thought and action.

To call on Shango begins with clarity of purpose. Sit quietly before his altar or a simple candle flame and focus on what you seek. If it is strength, imagine his lightning flowing through you; bright, controlled and alive. If it is justice, speak your truth aloud, trusting that Shango hears every word spoken with sincerity. His energy moves through sound and rhythm, so clapping, drumming, or even tapping your hand against your chest while praying helps align your heartbeat with his thunder. You may say:

"Shango, king of truth, master of fire, I call upon your light.

Let your flame burn within me, guiding my words and my actions.

Where fear lives, let courage rise.

Where injustice stands, let your lightning strike to reveal truth.

Oba Koso, may your justice reign!"

The words do not need to be perfect; what matters is the heart behind them. Speak with confidence, for Shango honors boldness and authenticity.

When calling upon Shango for justice, remember that he is not a god of vengeance but of balance. His fire restores order; it burns lies and pride, but it also protects the innocent and uplifts the righteous. If you have been wronged, ask him for clarity and resolution, not destruction. If you have wronged others, call upon his light to show you the path to atonement. Justice, to Shango, is about restoring harmony; not winning a battle, but ensuring truth prevails.

Some devotees choose to make offerings during their prayers, such as apples, roasted corn, or a few drops of rum carefully poured onto the ground or into a fireproof bowl. As the smoke rises, imagine your burdens lifting with it, your intentions carried to the heavens. Others may light red and white candles to represent strength and purity, or beat softly on a drum to mimic the rhythm of rain before a storm. Each action honors Shango's essence: sound, fire and transformation.

After your prayer, take a moment to sit in silence. Listen; not just with your ears, but with your spirit. Shango often answers through intuition, dreams, or sudden bursts of courage and clarity. His presence may come as warmth in your chest, a spark of insight, or an unexpected opportunity to act with truth.

To call on Shango is to step into your own fire; to awaken your courage, to act with integrity and to trust that justice, like thunder, always arrives when the world most needs to hear it.

Stories from Those Struck by Power

Those who walk with Shango often say that once he chooses you, you will know. His presence does not whisper; it roars. Yet within that thunder is a deep compassion, a guiding light that pushes his followers to rise above fear and stand in truth. To be "touched by lightning" is not always comfortable; it means transformation, awakening and sometimes being tested by fire. But those who have felt Shango's presence agree on one thing: his power changes everything.

One devotee, a drummer from Nigeria, spoke of how Shango came to him through rhythm. As a boy, he loved to play the *bàtá* drum but struggled to master the complex beats. During a festival, he became frustrated and stopped mid-performance. Suddenly, thunder rolled overhead and a bolt of lightning struck a nearby tree. The crowd gasped, but he felt no fear, only energy rushing through his body. From that day forward, his hands seemed to move on their own, flowing perfectly with every rhythm. He said, "It was as if the thunder taught me. I didn't just play for Shango anymore; I played *with* him."

A woman in Trinidad shared how Shango's fire guided her through injustice. Accused falsely at work, she prayed each night before her small altar, lighting a single red candle. Instead of asking for revenge, she asked for the truth to reveal itself. A week later, her employer discovered the real culprit and her name was cleared. She later said, "Shango didn't punish; he revealed. He showed me that justice is not about anger; it's about light." Her story became an example in her community, teaching others that devotion to Shango requires patience and trust in divine timing.

In Brazil, an elder priest of *Candomblé* described being healed by the energy of Shango. After years of illness, he began to feel his strength returning only when he resumed his duties at the temple, including dancing, drumming and teaching younger initiates about the Orisha. "When I danced again," he said, "I felt the lightning rise through my spine. Shango reminded me that my purpose was to serve. The sickness left when I returned to the flame." For him, the healing was not only physical but spiritual; a renewal of faith and duty.

Many devotees describe Shango's touch as both fire and calm. It comes as a spark of courage before a difficult decision, as thunder during a time of injustice, or as a steady flame during doubt. Some speak of dreams where they see him surrounded by light, his eyes like burning coals, reminding them to live with strength and honor.

These stories, from Africa to the Americas, share a common truth: Shango meets each devotee where they are but never leaves them as they were. His lightning does not destroy; it transforms. To be touched by him is to awaken the fire within, to find clarity in chaos and to live boldly in the truth that thunder itself walks beside you.

Sitting with the Flame Inside You

Meditating with Shango's fire is not a quiet escape from the world; it is an awakening within it. His flame burns not for comfort, but for clarity. When devotees sit before the light of a candle or the glow of a small fire, they are not simply observing heat and motion; they are gazing into a living symbol of divine truth. The goal of meditating in Shango's firelight is to align one's spirit with his courage, his integrity and his strength; to let the storm within find order and purpose.

Preparing for meditation begins with creating a sacred atmosphere. The space should be calm, clean and focused. Light a red or white candle on Shango's altar, or, if possible, sit near a safe flame outdoors. As the fire flickers, take a few deep breaths. Feel your heartbeat steady, echoing the rhythm of distant thunder. Speak his praise names softly to open the connection: *Kabiyesi Shango! Oba Koso!* Then allow silence to settle. Shango's lessons often arrive not through noise, but through awareness; the quiet after the storm.

The meditation itself centers on fire as both teacher and mirror. Watch the flame closely. See how it dances, yet remains anchored to its source. This is Shango's wisdom: power without grounding burns wildly, but balanced fire illuminates. Reflect on where your energy is focused in life. Are you letting emotions control you, or guiding them with discipline? Are your passions feeding growth or consuming peace? Shango's flame shows what needs transformation. As you breathe, imagine his lightning flowing through your body; burning away fear, pride and hesitation; leaving only truth and purpose behind.

During the meditation, devotees often repeat affirmations inspired by Shango's virtues. These words are not empty mantras; they are declarations of power, reshaping thought and intention. Some examples include:

- *"I carry the fire of truth within me."*
- *"My strength is steady, my will is just."*
- *"I act with courage and speak with honor."*
- *"Like lightning, I reveal what is hidden and stand in the light."*
- *"Shango's fire burns through my doubts and strengthens my heart."*

Repeating these affirmations aloud connects the body and voice to the divine rhythm. Each phrase is a spark, small but potent, reminding the soul of its divine potential.

After meditation, take a few moments to express gratitude. Offer a silent thank you to Shango for his guidance and extinguish the candle gently, never hastily. Reflect on any emotions, insights, or images that arose; these may be messages from the Orisha or truths your spirit is ready to face.

Over time, meditating in the firelight becomes a form of ongoing dialogue with Shango. It strengthens discipline, courage and clarity; the inner tools needed to live in alignment with his principles. His flame becomes a teacher, not of comfort, but of strength. And in its glow, you discover that the thunder's true home is within your own chest; the steady beat of a heart made fearless by divine fire.

When the Sky Sends a Message

Shango does not always speak in words; his messages arrive like thunder, sudden yet unmistakable. For those attuned to his energy, signs of his presence ripple through daily life in both grand and subtle ways. He is the fire that stirs your courage, the rhythm that guides your steps and the storm that clears away what no longer serves you. Shango is an Orisha who moves through experience, using life itself as his language. When he walks with you, even ordinary moments can crackle with divine meaning.

One of the most common ways Shango communicates is through synchronicity and timing. You might hear thunder right as you make a difficult decision or see flashes of lightning during a moment of truth. These are not coincidences; they are affirmations. Shango's storms often appear when justice is at play, when lies are exposed, or when courage is required. His presence reminds you that truth cannot stay hidden forever. In Yoruba tradition, lightning is not random; it is the voice of the Orisha declaring balance and change.

Shango also speaks through music, rhythm and sound. Hearing drums unexpectedly, or feeling drawn to a particular beat or song, can be his way of stirring your spirit. Some devotees claim that when they need direction, a sudden rhythm forms in their thoughts, almost like an echo of distant thunder, guiding them toward clarity. The sound of the *bàtá* drums, even if only remembered or imagined, can awaken strength and focus. When life feels heavy, Shango's rhythm calls the soul to move; to shake off stagnation and return to alignment.

In daily life, Shango's energy can manifest as moments of fiery emotion or inspiration. A sudden burst of confidence when speaking the truth, or a flash of righteous anger in the face of injustice, are not random feelings; they are the spark of his flame. He reminds you that passion, when guided by conscience, is sacred. His presence teaches balance: use the fire to build, not destroy; to defend truth, not pride.

For some, Shango's messages come through symbols and colors, with flashes of red and white, the discovery of axes, rams, or even the number six recurring. These are quiet confirmations of his guidance. In dreams, he may appear as a powerful man dressed in royal red, holding lightning in his hands, or standing in the rain surrounded by flame. His eyes may flash like fire, but his gaze carries wisdom, urging you to act with integrity and courage.

Above all, Shango's signs encourage action and accountability. He rarely calls for passive faith; instead, he pushes his followers to live their truth boldly. If you ask him for guidance, expect opportunities to demonstrate your strength and fairness. His lessons unfold through real-life challenges, teaching you to embody his fire rather than depend on it from afar.

When Shango speaks through the storm, he does so not to frighten, but to awaken. His signs are reminders that divine power moves through you, not around you. Every rumble of thunder, every moment of truth, is his way of saying: *Stand tall. Live justly. Burn bright.*

THE STORM THAT WILL NOT BE SILENCED

Borders have never contained Shango's fire. From the royal courts of ancient Oyo to the streets of Havana, Bahia, Port-au-Prince and beyond, his thunder still rolls across the world. His spirit traveled with those who carried his name in their hearts, surviving enslavement, exile and suppression to become a symbol of power, pride and resilience. Today, Shango's influence shines in music, art, activism and spiritual practice, reminding us that divine strength cannot be silenced. His fire burns in every act of truth and justice, in every drumbeat that honors ancestry and in every voice that rises against oppression.

The Spread of Shango's Influence

Shango's legacy did not remain in the land of Oyo; it crossed oceans, survived oppression and found new life wherever his followers were carried. When enslaved Africans were torn from their homeland, they brought with them more than memories; they carried faith, rhythm and the fire of their gods. Among them was Shango, the Orisha of thunder and justice, whose spirit could not be broken or silenced. His lightning struck across continents, taking root in new lands and shaping spiritual traditions from the Caribbean to the

Americas. Wherever his name was whispered, communities found strength, identity and a sense of resistance.

In West Africa, Shango was revered as both a king and a deity, a symbol of authority, courage and divine justice. When Yoruba people were captured and sold into slavery, they carried his stories, songs and rituals in their hearts. In foreign lands where their languages and traditions were forbidden, Shango's worship adapted to survive. His essence found expression through rhythm, dance and symbols that transcended words. Even when the name "Shango" could not be spoken aloud, his thunder was felt in the heartbeat of the drum and the strength of the people who remembered him.

In Cuba, his legacy emerged through *Santería*, where he became known as *Changó*. Enslaved Africans disguised their devotion under the image of Catholic saints, associating Shango with Saint Barbara, whose lightning and sword mirrored his own power. Yet beneath this disguise, his true spirit remained vibrant. His festivals, offerings and rhythms continued in secret, passed down through generations. Over time, *Changó* became one of the most celebrated Orishas in the Caribbean, representing not only power and passion but also resilience in the face of adversity.

In Brazil, he transformed into *Xangô*, honored in the traditions of *Candomblé* and *Umbanda*. His worship grew into public celebrations, marked by drums, fire and dance echoing his thunderous might. The Brazilian people embraced his dual nature as warrior and judge, protector and purifier. Temples devoted to *Xangô* still stand across Bahia and Pernambuco, their altars glowing with candles and offerings of red and white.

In Trinidad and Tobago, *Shango Baptists* carried his legacy through a blend of Yoruba spirituality and Christianity. Despite years of persecution, their faith survived underground until it was finally recognized and celebrated as part of the nation's cultural identity. His name also lives in the chants of *Vodou* in Haiti, where his energy merges with spirits of fire and thunder, continuing his role as a divine force of justice.

Through centuries of displacement and change, Shango's fire adapted without losing its essence. His influence now extends beyond religion into music, art and activism. He represents empowerment, leadership and the unyielding will to stand tall against injustice.

Shango's lightning continues to flash across continents, reminding all who honor him that divine power cannot be contained. It moves where it must, transforming, uniting and illuminating those who carry the flame of courage and truth in every corner of the world.

Shango in Justice Movements

Shango has always been more than an Orisha of thunder; he is a living symbol of resistance, truth and divine justice. Across centuries, his fire has ignited not only altars but hearts determined to challenge injustice. In the diaspora, where African traditions were suppressed, Shango's image became a quiet protest and later a roaring voice for freedom. His thunder rolled through the drums of rebellion, the songs of survival and the movements of people demanding dignity. As a god of power and protest, Shango stands as both a protector and an awakener, reminding humanity that justice is not granted; it must be claimed with courage.

In the days of slavery, Shango's energy fueled rebellion. His worship was forbidden, yet his name was whispered among the enslaved as a promise that the oppressor's power was not absolute. His storms became metaphors for uprising; the unstoppable force of nature that no chain could restrain. In Haiti, echoes of Shango's might resonated through the Vodou spirit Ogoun, god of war and freedom, during the Haitian Revolution. The fire that burned in those who fought for liberation bore the same essence: Shango's flame of righteous defiance.

In the Caribbean, Shango's energy evolved into a cultural heartbeat for identity and pride. In Trinidad, the *Shango Baptist* faith emerged as both a spiritual path and a statement of resistance. Practitioners faced persecution and ridicule for decades, yet they refused to silence their drums or abandon their prayers. Every rhythm played and every hymn sung became a declaration: *we are still here and our gods are still with us.* When the religion was finally legalized in the mid-20th century, it marked not only spiritual recognition but the triumph of endurance; a victory that Shango himself would have celebrated as justice fulfilled.

In Brazil, *Xangô*'s influence reached beyond the temples of *Candomblé*. He became a cultural emblem for Afro-Brazilian empowerment and a symbol of truth in the face of oppression. Songs praising Xangô found their way into samba, capoeira and even political movements, reminding people that power can be righteous and that divine fire burns in every act of courage. The Orisha's message of balance, strength guided by wisdom, became a foundation for social justice and community leadership.

In modern times, Shango's spirit continues to inspire activists, artists and thinkers across the African diaspora. His thunder echoes in the rhythms of protest marches, in the chants for equality and in the raised voices of those who refuse to bow to injustice. For many, Shango represents divine accountability; the truth that even the mighty are answerable to moral law.

Shango's legacy as a god of power and protest teaches that fire, when guided by conscience, can become a transformative force. His example calls every generation to stand firm, to speak the truth without fear and to face injustice with the strength of a thunderstorm. Through him, we are reminded that divine power is not domination; it is the courage to rise, resist and restore balance where the world has fallen silent.

Fire That Redefines the Masculine

Shango stands as one of the most complex representations of masculinity in the Yoruba pantheon; strong, passionate, commanding, yet deeply emotional and capable of love and mercy. His fire does not exist to dominate but to illuminate. Through him, we see a vision of sacred masculinity that transcends stereotypes of aggression and control. Shango's power lies in balance: he embodies both the warrior and the lover, the leader and the learner, the thunder and the silence. In a world often uncertain about what true strength means, Shango's example offers a path of integrity, vulnerability and purpose; a reimagining of what it means to be powerful with conscience.

In Yoruba tradition, masculinity is not defined solely by force, but by *iwà pẹ̀lẹ́*, which encompasses good character and self-mastery. Shango, though fierce and proud, learns this lesson through his own mythic journey. His temper once caused destruction, yet his willingness to grow transformed him into a divine judge and protector. His story demonstrates that being masculine is not about suppressing emotions or exerting control; it is about learning balance, taking responsibility and using strength for the benefit of others. His dual nature, both fire and justice, teaches that emotional depth and moral clarity are signs of maturity, not weakness.

Across the African diaspora, Shango's image became a symbol of cultural and personal empowerment. In Cuba, Brazil and Trinidad, his presence inspired men to reclaim pride in their African heritage and spiritual strength. Under colonial systems that tried to strip Black men of dignity and identity, Shango's thunder reminded them that power was still theirs; that divine masculinity did not come from domination, but from resilience, leadership and love for community. His red and white colors represented not only fire and purity but also courage and balance; an ideal to live by rather than a mask to wear.

In modern times, Shango's archetype challenges rigid definitions of gender. His connection to female Orishas, such as Oya, Oshun and

Obba, highlights the sacred interplay between masculine and feminine energies. He depends on them not as subordinates but as equals, partners in creation and power. Their stories together illustrate that divine balance requires cooperation and respect. This harmony presents a powerful model for humanity, demonstrating that true masculinity encompasses partnership, empathy and emotional intelligence without compromising strength.

For many men today, especially in Afro-diasporic spiritual paths, walking with Shango means healing inherited wounds about identity. It means learning that vulnerability and discipline can coexist, that leadership can be gentle yet firm and that love can be fierce without harm. Women and non-binary devotees also find empowerment in his energy, connecting to the assertive and protective aspects within themselves. Shango's fire burns beyond gender; it represents the sacred potential of all who act with courage and truth.

Through Shango, masculinity is reborn not as dominance but as devotion; a flame that protects, uplifts and transforms. His thunder calls each of us, regardless of gender, to live with honor and authenticity, proving that true strength is not about control, but about the wisdom to wield power with heart.

The Beat That Keeps Him Alive

Shango's fire has always belonged to those who dare to live boldly and in today's world, that fire burns brightest in the hearts of the young. Across continents, new generations are rediscovering his thunder through music, art, activism and spirituality. The Orisha who once ruled ancient Oyo now inspires a digital age, where his message of courage, justice and truth continues to guide those seeking identity and empowerment. For the youth of the African diaspora, Shango's drums are more than rhythm; they are heartbeat and heritage, calling them to remember who they are and to carry the storm forward.

In many communities, young people are rediscovering ancestral traditions that were once dismissed or suppressed. Through Shango, they find strength and a sense of belonging. His story, of pride, downfall and transformation, mirrors their own struggles to navigate a complex world while staying true to their roots. He teaches them that mistakes do not define destiny; what matters is rising again, wiser and stronger. In an era when many are reclaiming their cultural and spiritual identities, Shango becomes a symbol of revival; a reminder that African wisdom is not a relic of the past, but a living flame guiding the future.

Shango's influence on youth culture is visible in music and performance. The rhythms once played on *bàtá* drums now pulse through hip-hop, reggae, samba and Afrobeat. Modern musicians invoke his name in lyrics about justice and power, blending traditional chants with contemporary beats. In these spaces, the thunder still speaks; shaping art that challenges inequality, celebrates pride and builds bridges between past and present. Every beat is a prayer; every dance is resistance. Through rhythm, young people transform creativity into activism, echoing Shango's legacy of truth and defiance.

Beyond music, his energy also fuels social movements led by youth who fight against oppression, racism and environmental harm. His flame represents the courage to speak truth to power, to confront corruption and to demand accountability. Many who study his teachings see him not just as a divine figure, but as a symbol of moral leadership. His fire teaches that strength must serve justice, that passion must be guided by conscience and that silence in the face of injustice dishonors the divine within.

This revival of Shango's fire is also happening within spiritual communities. Young devotees are learning the traditional chants, dances and rituals, ensuring that ancient knowledge continues to thrive. Through online spaces and cultural festivals, they share his teachings with global audiences, connecting tradition to modern life. Their devotion reclaims what history tried to erase, reminding the world that the flame of Shango will never fade so long as even one heart beats to his rhythm.

Shango's thunder is timeless. It rolls across generations, calling each one to rise with integrity and pride. The youth who answer his call are not merely keeping tradition alive; they are transforming it, turning ancestral rhythm into the sound of renewal. Through them, the storm continues. Through them, the fire still burns.

BECOMING THE STORM AND THE SHELTER

To live the storm is to walk with purpose, strength and truth; the way of Shango himself. His wisdom is not meant to remain on altars or in stories; it is meant to move through daily life. Shango teaches that real power is not domination but integrity, that fire is sacred when guided by conscience. To embody his energy is to live with courage, to speak boldly and to stand firm in justice even when the sky trembles. His lessons remind us that every challenge is a forge, every storm a teacher. To live the storm is to live awake; to become lightning in motion, transforming not through destruction, but through the light of truth.

Lead Like Fire Without Burning the World

To lead like lightning is to move with clarity, purpose and truth. Shango's leadership is not loud for the sake of noise; it is powerful because it strikes with precision. Lightning does not wander; it knows exactly where to go, illuminating everything it touches. Similarly, Shango teaches that true leadership begins with focus and integrity. It is not about ruling others but guiding them through example. Those who follow his path learn that to lead is to embody truth; to let light cut through confusion and stand firm even when storms surround them.

In Yoruba tradition, Shango's kingship was not given lightly. He earned it through strength, intelligence and vision. Yet, his rule was not without trials. His fiery temper once brought chaos, reminding us that strength without balance leads to downfall. His redemption, rising from his mistakes to become a divine Orisha, shows that great leaders are not perfect, but accountable. They face their flaws, learn from them and grow stronger. Shango's lightning teaches that leadership is forged through humility as much as power.

To lead like lightning, one must first know the truth. Shango's energy does not tolerate falsehood. He teaches that a leader's words carry weight and must be used to uplift, not deceive. Truth is the foundation of every decision, whether in family, community, or spiritual life. Like lightning, it may be blinding at first, but it clears the air, allowing new growth to begin. To live by truth is to align with divine order; to honor Àṣẹ, the life force that keeps the universe in balance.

The second lesson is strength, not as brute force, but as courage. Shango's strength is both external and internal. It defends the weak, speaks out against injustice and holds firm in its convictions. Yet, it also means having the courage to admit wrongs, to stand alone when necessary and to choose peace when anger tempts destruction. His fire burns brightest when guided by wisdom. A true leader does not hide from challenges but meets them head-on, knowing that storms refine rather than ruin.

Finally, Shango embodies clarity in action. Just as lightning lights the path for a moment, leadership requires vision; the ability to see what others may miss. This clarity is born from reflection, discipline and connection to spirit. Shango's devotees learn to pause before acting, channeling their emotions into a purposeful direction. Decisions made in haste can burn, but those guided by insight illuminate.

In modern life, to lead like lightning means carrying Shango's wisdom into every role you play: parent, teacher, healer, activist and artist. It means speaking with honesty, acting with courage and refusing to let fear silence your truth. Shango's lightning does not destroy; it transforms. It reveals what is hidden and energizes what is true. To lead in one's own way is to become that light in the storm; a presence that inspires others not by control, but by example, reminding them that real power is born from clarity, justice and a genuine heart.

Turning Rage into Righteousness

Shango's fire is not wild; it burns with purpose. His flame does not exist to consume but to transform, to turn passion into power and power into legacy. For those who follow his path, this is one of his greatest lessons: that energy without direction fades, but when guided by wisdom, it can illuminate generations to come. To live with Shango's fire is to act with intention; to create, to protect and to build something that endures beyond the self.

Passion, like fire, begins as a spark. It fills the heart with energy, drive and desire. Yet Shango teaches that passion alone is not enough. Without focus, it can scatter or even be destroyed. The challenge is to give that fire purpose; to connect it to truth, vision and service. Shango's devotees often say that his energy inspires them to move forward, to break free from stagnation and to live boldly. But his flame also demands responsibility. He asks, *"What are you creating with the fire I have given you?"*

Shango's own story is a testament to this principle. As a mortal king, he was known for his charisma, confidence and fierce will. His passions inspired loyalty, but at times, they also led to mistakes. It was only through reflection and transformation that he turned his fire from destruction to enlightenment. When he ascended as an Orisha, his flame became sacred; no longer personal ambition, but divine purpose. Through him, we learn that legacy begins when passion serves something greater than ego.

To turn passion into legacy, Shango calls us to align our energy with our values. Every skill, talent, or dream becomes meaningful when connected to justice, creativity, or community. For some, that means building families rooted in love and integrity. For others, it may be creating art, teaching truth, or standing for fairness in a world that often rewards deceit. Shango's fire asks us to act, not only for ourselves but for those who will come after. The flame we tend today becomes the light that guides others tomorrow.

His devotees often express this in daily life through ritual and action. Lighting candles, speaking affirmations, or performing small acts of courage all help to fuel the flame of purpose. A musician may channel Shango's rhythm through their drums; a teacher may carry his voice in every lesson about integrity; a leader may embody his justice in every decision. Passion finds meaning when it becomes service; when it uplifts others and honors the divine spark within.

Ultimately, Shango's message is simple yet profound: *Do not waste your fire.* Every heartbeat, every talent, every moment of inspiration is an opportunity to create a lasting legacy. His flame reminds us that power is sacred when it builds, heals and inspires. To live with fire in Shango's way is to be a maker of light; to turn passion into action and action into a legacy that continues to burn long after the storm has passed.

Keeping the Fire Lit at Your Doorstep

Shango's fire is not meant to burn only in temples or ceremonies; it belongs in everyday life. His presence thrives where there is rhythm, honesty and courage and these qualities can live in every home. To honor Shango daily is to carry his flame not just on the altar, but in the way you speak, act and create. Living devotion means transforming ordinary routines into sacred expressions of balance, discipline and joy. When your home becomes a reflection of his energy, you do not simply worship Shango; you *live* with him.

Bringing Shango's flame into your home begins with intention. Keep his space clean, bright and active. Light a candle in his colors: red for power, white for clarity, each morning or evening. As the flame flickers, take a moment to speak a short prayer or affirmation: *"May my actions today be just and my heart courageous."* This simple ritual reminds you that divine fire lives within you, guiding each decision. Grand gestures do not measure devotion, but by consistency; the willingness to show up daily with truth and gratitude.

Music and rhythm are also essential for living in harmony with Shango's energy. Drumming, clapping, or even listening to lively percussion connects your spirit to his thunder. You can honor him while cooking, cleaning, or working by humming his songs or moving with the rhythm of your heartbeat. Every motion becomes an offering. Joy and movement, please Shango, because they reflect vitality; the fire of life in motion. A home filled with laughter and purpose is one he blesses.

Acts of integrity are another form of devotion. Shango is the guardian of justice and his fire burns brightest in those who live truthfully. Be fair in your words, reliable in your promises and humble in your victories. If conflict arises, seek a resolution rather than seeking revenge. When you correct wrongdoing or stand up for someone who has been mistreated, you honor Shango as surely as if you lit a candle in his name. Living by his principles turns your actions into prayers.

Food, too, can be a way of devotion. Preparing meals with gratitude, especially those connected to his offerings, like apples, corn, okra, or spicy dishes, invites his energy into your home. Sharing food with others, feeding the hungry, or simply giving thanks before eating are acts that extend his generosity into daily life. His fire nourishes not only the body but also the bonds between people.

Above all, Shango's flame in the home means keeping your spirit alive. It is about courage during hardship, joy during uncertainty and balance amid chaos. His presence teaches that devotion is not separation from life; it is a deeper engagement with it. When your words are honest, your actions deliberate and your heart steady, Shango's energy flows through your home like steady firelight. His flame reminds you that even the tiniest spark of integrity can illuminate the world. To live with Shango's fire daily is to let every moment, no matter how small, burn with purpose and divine truth.

Be Fierce Be Kind Be True

To walk the path of Shango is to learn the sacred balance between storm and stillness. He is thunder and calm, fire and light, power and protection. To "be the storm" means to embody his strength; to stand tall in truth, to challenge injustice and to move boldly when change is needed. To "be the shelter" means to embody his mercy; to offer safety, understanding and compassion to those around you. Together, these two forces form the essence of Shango's wisdom: strength guided by heart.

In Yoruba tradition, the Orisha are not distant gods; they are living principles of nature and character. To walk their path is to live in alignment with their energy. Shango's energy is dynamic; it is the power to act with courage and fairness in all circumstances. When life demands action, his thunder reminds us not to hide from challenge. When life requires patience, his fire teaches us restraint. He is the rhythm that keeps us balanced between passion and purpose.

To be the storm is to confront life with conviction. It means refusing to remain silent in the face of injustice and using your voice to bring truth into the open. Shango's followers are taught to carry themselves with dignity, to lead with courage and to take decisive action when needed. His fire is not reckless; it burns through fear, not reason. When you channel his storm, you become a force for transformation: challenging falsehood, shaking complacency and sparking growth in yourself and others. His lightning does not destroy without cause; it strikes where clarity is needed most.

But to walk only as the storm is to forget Shango's other face. To be the shelter means to temper strength with compassion. It is essential to remember that thunder both protects and awakens. Shango teaches that power is sacred only when it defends, not dominates. Being the shelter means creating peace in your relationships, offering support to those in pain and using your fire to warm rather than scorch. The true devotee of Shango understands that the most powerful storms also bring rain, the blessing that nourishes and restores.

In daily life, walking Shango's path means finding this harmony within yourself. When anger arises, let it speak truth but not cruelty. When power comes, let it uplift, not oppress. When others stumble, be the steady flame that lights the way. In doing so, you mirror the Orisha's own evolution, from a passionate king to a divine embodiment of justice and wisdom.

To walk with Shango is to live awake; to know when to roar and when to listen, when to strike and when to shield. His path teaches that strength and compassion are not opposites but allies. When your heart burns with truth and your actions honor fairness, you become both the storm and the shelter. You become living thunder; power guided by grace, fire tempered by love and proof that divine balance can dwell in human form.

CONCLUSION
LEAVING FOOTPRINTS IN THE STORM

To walk with Shango is to carry both thunder and light within you. His energy is not only a force of destruction or power; it is the pulse of creation, rhythm and truth. Shango reminds us that fire, when guided by conscience, becomes a path toward balance and enlightenment. His legacy burns through time, crossing oceans, generations and hearts, calling all who seek justice, courage and integrity to rise and live with purpose. As we reach the end of this journey through his stories, symbols and wisdom, we find that walking with thunder is not about worshiping from afar; it is about embodying his lessons daily, letting his flame ignite the strength and honor that dwell within every soul.

The Hand That Strikes and Soothes

Shango is power incarnate, yet his might is never without compassion. His lightning strikes to reveal truth, not to destroy mindlessly. His thunder shatters silence but restores order. Through his dual nature, we see that divine strength is always paired with mercy. To follow him is to understand that power without grace is incomplete.

In the myths of his life, Shango's fire once burned out of control; his temper caused suffering and his pride brought downfall. Yet from that fall came transformation. When he ascended to the heavens, he became not just the god of thunder but the guardian of justice, learning that leadership requires humility and love. He who once struck without restraint became the one who heals through clarity and fairness. This journey from fury to wisdom is at the heart of Shango's grace; it shows that even the strongest must learn tenderness.

For his devotees, this balance becomes a spiritual compass. Shango teaches that we can wield influence without cruelty, passion without recklessness and authority without arrogance. His fire challenges us to confront our flaws honestly and transform them into a source of strength. When you act with his integrity, you become a mirror of divine justice; bold yet kind, powerful yet compassionate. His thunder becomes a cleansing rain, washing away falsehood and awakening truth.

To embrace Shango's grace is to remember that healing often follows upheaval. Just as the earth grows greener after the storm, so too does the spirit grow stronger after a challenge. His energy reminds us that destruction is not always an end, but sometimes the beginning of renewal.

Wisdom Forged in Fire and Thunder

Through Shango's stories, we have seen that power must serve truth, that leadership requires humility and that emotion, when balanced by wisdom, becomes a sacred force. His myths are more than tales of gods and kings; they are lessons on human nature.

From his *double-headed axe*, we learn the duality of justice: every action cuts two ways and every choice carries consequences. From his colors, red and white, we know that passion and purity must coexist.

From his storms, we understand that chaos can cleanse and that growth often follows conflict.

We also learn that strength is not the absence of vulnerability. Shango's love for Oya, Oshun and Obba teaches that emotion is not a weakness, but a connection. His heart, full of both desire and compassion, reveals that masculinity rooted in empathy is a sacred quality. He reminds men and women alike that true power does not suppress emotion; it channels it into purpose.

From Shango's fire, we learn transformation. Fire consumes, yes, but it also renews. It turns wood to ash and ash to soil, allowing new life to emerge. Shango's fire burns away deceit, pride and fear, leaving only what is real. To walk with him is to welcome change and to trust that even loss carries the seed of rebirth.

Finally, we learn from his rhythm. Shango's thunder is not random; it follows divine order. His drumming represents the heartbeat of the universe, teaching that all creation moves in balance. The wise learn to listen; to find that rhythm in their own lives and align their steps with it. When we dance to Shango's rhythm, we remember that life, like music, is not about perfection but harmony.

Carrying the Flame into Tomorrow

To live as Shango's devotee today is to bring his principles into a world often clouded by confusion and injustice. You do not need to wear his crown to reflect his fire; it lives in the way you walk, speak and act. His energy belongs not only to temples or rituals but to every moment of truth and courage in daily life.

Living with his fire means standing firm in your values, even when the world tests them. It means speaking truth even when silence would be easier. Shango's devotees are not passive; they are doers, creators and protectors. When you choose fairness over greed, compassion over cruelty, or justice over comfort, you live his teachings.

Modern life often praises speed and ambition, but Shango's fire reminds us that power without direction burns out quickly. To live his way is to channel energy with intention. Every action becomes meaningful when performed with awareness, whether at work, in creation, or while helping others. His lessons inspire us to pursue excellence without ego, to lead without domination and to love without fear.

Even in small acts, Shango's presence can be felt. Lighting a candle before beginning your day, offering a moment of gratitude for truth, or keeping your word when no one is watching; these are acts of devotion. His fire lives wherever honesty, courage and balance thrive.

In a world that often mistakes noise for strength, Shango reminds us that real power is quiet confidence; the lightning that shines only long enough to show the path. He teaches that fire in the heart must be tempered with clarity in the mind. His devotees are both warriors and peacemakers, protectors of justice and bringers of joy.

To live as his follower is to hold that sacred balance; to be unafraid to strike when truth demands it, yet humble enough to shelter others in compassion. It is to embody thunder and stillness, passion and peace, turning life itself into a ritual of integrity.

Step Into the Storm With Open Eyes

The legacy of Shango is not one of worship alone; it is a call to action. His thunder invites every soul to rise and live fearlessly, to take ownership of their choices and to shape the world with justice and heart. He does not ask for perfection; he asks for courage. He does not demand obedience; he calls for authenticity.

To go forth with thunder is to live awake; to move through life with your spirit ignited. When challenges come, face them like Shango faced the storm: not with fear, but with purpose. When injustice arises, let your voice be strong, but your hand guided by fairness. When blessings arrive, share them freely, for Shango's greatness was never selfish; it was generous, inspiring others to rise.

Carry his lessons into every part of your life. Be the spark that lights hope in others, the storm that shakes complacency and the calm after that restores peace. Let your words carry truth, your actions reflect honor and your presence inspire strength.

Remember that walking with thunder means embracing both light and shadow; the power to act and the wisdom to pause. It is knowing when to speak and when to listen, when to lead and when to serve. It is living in such a way that your fire becomes not destruction, but guidance for those who follow.

Shango's legacy lives wherever courage meets compassion, wherever truth burns brighter than fear. The thunder that once echoed across the skies of Oyo now beats in the hearts of all who honor him; in every rhythm of resistance, every act of justice, every flame of integrity.

Go forth, then, with thunder in your heart and light in your hands. Walk boldly, live justly and burn bright. For Shango's fire is not only around you; it is within you. And when you live in truth, the world will hear it, not as a whisper, but as the voice of thunder itself.

Feeling stuck, drained, or tested?

It's time to connect with a power that doesn't break, it builds. Aganjú: Voice of the Volcano is your guide to grounding, healing, and transformation through one of the most ancient forces in African spirituality.

Learn how to honor Aganjú through rituals, offerings, and daily practices that awaken resilience from the inside out.

Whether you're new to Orisha traditions or deepening your path, this book offers practical tools for navigating life's most challenging moments with strength and serenity.

Get your copy now and let the fire within rise.

BIBLIOGRAPHY

Abimbola, W. (1975). *Ifá: An exposition of Ifá literary corpus.* Oxford University Press.
Abiodun, R. (2014). *Yoruba art and language: Seeking the African in African art.* Cambridge University Press.
Adegbite, A. (1988). *The impact of Yoruba traditional music on Nigerian popular music.* University of Ibadan Press.
Adogame, A., Chitando, E., & Bateye, B. (Eds.). (2012). *African traditions in the study of religion, diaspora and gendered societies.* Routledge.
Adefarakan, T. (2018). *Afrospiritual aesthetics: The orisha, Yoruba cosmology and the arts.* Lexington Books.
Aiyejina, F. (1999). The Shango cult in Trinidad: Religion, identity and cultural resistance. *Caribbean Quarterly*, 45(2), 25–40.
Ajayi, J. F. A. (Ed.). (1998). *General history of Africa: Volume VI – Africa in the nineteenth century until the 1880s.* UNESCO Publishing.
Barnes, S. T. (1997). *Africa's Ogun: Old world and new (2nd ed.).* Indiana University Press.
Bascom, W. R. (1969). *The Yoruba of southwestern Nigeria.* Holt, Rinehart and Winston.
Beier, U. (1956). *The return of Shango: Studies in Yoruba religion.* Black Orpheus Press.
Brandon, G. (1993). *Santería from Africa to the New World: The dead sell memories.* Indiana University Press.
Brown, D. H. (2003). *Santería enthroned: Art, ritual and innovation in an Afro-Cuban religion.* University of Chicago Press.
Clarke, K. (2004). *Mapping Yoruba networks: Power and agency in the making of transnational communities.* Duke University Press.
Drewal, H. J. (1992). *Yoruba ritual: Performers, play, agency.* Indiana University Press.
Falola, T., & Genova, A. (2005). *Yoruba identity and power politics.* University of Rochester Press.
Hagedorn, K. J. (2001). *Divine utterances: The performance of Afro-Cuban Santería.* Smithsonian Institution Press.
Idowu, E. B. (1962). *Olodumare: God in Yoruba belief.* Longman.
Mason, J. (1992). *Orin Orisha: Songs for selected heads.* Yoruba Theological Archministry.
Matory, J. L. (2005). *Black Atlantic religion: Tradition, transnationalism and matriarchy in the Afro-Brazilian Candomblé.* Princeton University Press.
McCarthy Brown, K. (1991). *Mama Lola: A Vodou priestess in Brooklyn.* University of California Press.
Murphy, J. M. (1993). *Santería: African spirits in America.* Beacon Press.
Olupona, J. K. (Ed.). (2014). *City of 201 gods: Ilé-Ifẹ̀ in time, space and the imagination.* University of California Press.

Pemberton, J. (1975). *Eshu-Elegba: The Yoruba trickster god.* African Arts, 9(1), 60–67.
Stewart, C. (2005). *Syncretism and its synonyms: Reflections on cultural mixture.* Diacritics, 35(2), 40–62.
Thompson, R. F. (1983). *Flash of the spirit: African and Afro-American art and philosophy.* Random House.

ABOUT THE AUTHOR

Monique Joiner Siedlak is a writer, witch, and warrior on a mission to awaken people to their greatest potential through the power of storytelling infused with mysticism, modern paganism, and new age spirituality. At the young age of 12, she began rigorously studying the fascinating philosophy of Wicca. By the time she was 20, she was self-initiated into the craft, and hasn't looked back ever since. To this day, she has authored over 50 books pertaining to the magick and mysteries of life.

To find out more about Monique Joiner Siedlak artistically, spiritually, and personally, feel free to visit her **official website**.

www.mojosiedlak.com

facebook.com/mojosiedlak

x.com/mojosiedlak

instagram.com/mojosiedlak

pinterest.com/mojosiedlak

youtube.com/@MoniqueJoinerSiedlak_Author

bookbub.com/authors/monique-joiner-siedlak

ALSO BY THE AUTHOR

African Spirituality Beliefs and Practices
Hoodoo

Seven African Powers: The Orishas

Cooking for the Orishas

Lucumi: The Ways of Santeria

Voodoo of Louisiana

Haitian Vodou

Orishas of Trinidad

Connecting with your Ancestors

Blood Magick

The Orishas

Vodun: West Africa's Spiritual Life

Marie Laveau: Life of a Voodoo Queen

Candomblé: Dancing for the God

Umbanda

Exploring the Rich and Diverse World of African Spirituality

African Shamanism: The Power of Spiritual Healing and Transformation

www.ingramcontent.com/pod-product-compliance
Lightning Source LLC
LaVergne TN
LVHW051243080426
835513LV00016B/1719